Archibald P.P. Rosebery

Appreciations and Addresses

Second Edition

Archibald P.P. Rosebery

Appreciations and Addresses
Second Edition

ISBN/EAN: 9783337075309

Printed in Europe, USA, Canada, Australia, Japan

Cover: Foto ©ninafisch / pixelio.de

More available books at **www.hansebooks.com**

· EARL · OF · ROSEBERY · · K · G ·

APPRECIATIONS AND ADDRESSES

DELIVERED BY

LORD ROSEBERY

EDITED BY

CHARLES GEAKE

JOHN LANE
LONDON AND NEW YORK
MDCCCXCIX

SECOND EDITION

Printed by BALLANTYNE, HANSON & Co.
London & Edinburgh

EDITOR'S NOTE

Lord Rosebery has said that "there were a hundred Mr. Gladstones." If there are not quite so many Lord Roseberys, it is at all events undeniable that there are a very considerable number. To decide how many might provoke discussion, and even excite controversy; it is happily only necessary here to state that from this volume one Lord Rosebery, and one only, has been excluded—Lord Rosebery the politician. This is not, it should at once be added, in censure of his politics, but in explanation of the principle deliberately adopted in selecting the speeches which constitute these "Appreciations and Addresses."

All the speeches, too, are of comparatively recent date, and all except two have been delivered since the memorable Liberal meeting at Edinburgh when Lord Rosebery shook the dust of leadership off his feet. They have been made under very different conditions,

EDITOR'S NOTE

and in very varying circumstances. There is the funeral oration in which Lord Rosebery paid fitting tribute to his great leader, colleague, and friend, Mr. Gladstone; the commemorative address, such as the two Appreciations of Burns; the chairman's running commentary on the delivered lecture, as is to be found in "London" and "Parliamentary Oratory"; the public function speech, such as inevitably accompanies the opening of a meeting, a public library, or even a golf-club house; and the purely post-prandial utterance such as the eulogy of "Sport" uttered to the Gimcracks. But all have been included, as parts of the whole, and as illustrating and elucidating their author's many-sidedness.

In one of them he speaks of the "miracle called Burns"; there are critics of his own who talk of the "mystery called Rosebery." There is, however, very little that is mysterious about these "Appreciations and Addresses," unless, indeed, it be the fact that they are all so uniformly interesting. This is not in immodest praise of the Editor's discrimination in selecting these particular speeches, but a recognition of the fact that whatever Lord Rosebery says or does always is of profound interest. It is said that a politician measures his place in popular esteem by the category into which

EDITOR'S NOTE

he is placed by the Press, ever ready to give the public what it wants. To be a "one column" man is evidence of a respectable position; to be reported verbatim the sign and seal of supreme distinction. Lord Rosebery belongs to the very small and select verbatim class; indeed, there is such eagerness shown on occasions that the demand overleaps the supply, and he is, alas! credited with more than he has actually said. But reading between the lines is a delicate and dangerous operation which he has himself deprecated, and the reader may be assured that the "Appreciations and Addresses" are in no sense the result of any imagination, "boiling" or otherwise—except it be Lord Rosebery's own.

As to the responsibility for this present volume, all that need be said is that Lord Rosebery undoubtedly made the speeches. In such a case as his it is more than the written word that remains; and, whatever his own personal view may chance to be of the result, the Editor says the conventional, "Go, little book" with much more than the conventional amount of confidence.

C. G.

CONTENTS

APPRECIATIONS

	PAGE
BURKE	5
ROBERT BURNS	31
WALLACE	73
ROBERT LOUIS STEVENSON	89
GLADSTONE	105
LONDON	123

ADDRESSES

BOOKISHNESS AND STATESMANSHIP	141
THE DUTY OF PUBLIC SERVICE	173
OUR CIVIL SERVANTS	207
THE QUALITY OF JUDGMENT	221
THE WORK OF PUBLIC LIBRARIES	235
PARLIAMENTARY ORATORY	247
THE ENGLISH-SPEAKING BROTHERHOOD	261
SCOTTISH HISTORY	273
ETON	287
THE HAPPY TOWN COUNCILLOR	301
SPORT	307
GOLF	323

APPRECIATIONS

BURKE

The first of these Appreciations of Burke was delivered at Bristol on October 30th, 1894, at a time when Lord Rosebery was Prime Minister. The occasion was the unveiling of a statue to Burke, the work of a Bristol sculptor, Mr. Havard Thomas. Continuous rain prevented the actual unveiling ceremony being anything more than merely formal, with the result that Lord Rosebery's speech was delivered at the Colston Hall.

The second Appreciation was delivered on July 7th, 1898, at Hall Barn, where a distinguished company were entertained at luncheon by Sir Edward Lawson, after a memorial to Burke had been unveiled by Lord Rosebery in the church of St. Mary and All Saints, Beaconsfield. The memorial consists of two panels— the upper containing a portrait of Burke, the lower the following inscription: "Edmund Burke, patriot, orator, statesman, lived at Butler's Court, formerly Gregories, in this parish, from 1769 to 1797. This memorial, placed here by public subscription, records the undying honour in which his name is held."

BURKE

I

WE rejoice that this statue, which we consecrate to-day to the memory of one of the greatest inhabitants of the United Kingdom, was given, not from outside, not from America, as those statues are sometimes given, but by a Bristol man to wipe out an unfortunate Bristol memory. Fellow citizens, it is a great honour for me to be here. It would have been a great honour for me to come here as a simple guest on such an occasion, but as a central figure I find it somewhat overmuch. There is indeed one of my colleagues, Mr. John Morley—whose consummate book on Burke is probably familiar to you—who would have unveiled this statue and delivered an admirable discourse with little or no trouble

APPRECIATIONS

to himself and with the greatest satisfaction to his audience. But a person who holds the office that I occupy is the very worst person to call upon for a function of this kind, because he is so embedded in the present, so tied and pegged down to the actual work of the day, that it is difficult for him, even in his moments of relaxation, to take one delightful excursion into the regions of the past. I could not, however, resist the instance of your eminent fellow citizen who has put up this statue, and I come therefore with the utmost zeal, but with a due sense of my own imperfections, to place my rude wreath at the foot of the statue which I have uncovered to-day.

We meet to-day to fulfil a tardy act of expiation. It is about 114 years since Bristol dismissed Edmund Burke from her service. She has long since repented that dismissal. She repents it to-day, not in sheet and with candle, not in dust and ashes, but in the nobler and more significant form of that effigy which has been unveiled outside. It is well to be a great city. It is well to have your port filled with the commerce of the seas. But it is better to be able to own that you have been in the wrong and to put up a signal monument of acknowledgment. But there is this to be remembered on the other side. Bristol gave Burke the greatest honour that Burke had ever received, for in what we call honours, contemporary honours, the career of Burke was singularly deficient. A subordinate office in the Government, a pension or two, the Rectorship of a Scottish University, about represent all that Burke received of official honour in his lifetime. But Bristol returned Burke unsolicited, as Yorkshire returned Brougham; and when we remember that the representation of Yorkshire was more to Brougham than the woolsack, we may measure without difficulty what Bristol was to Burke. Brougham, in a moment of unwisdom, left Yorkshire for the woolsack. But Burke would never have left Bristol of his own accord, for he well knew the strength and power that is given to a public man when he stands forward, not on his own merits, but as the representative of a great public constituency. And in those days great popular

APPRECIATIONS

constituencies were infinitely rarer than they are now, and Bristol was then the second city of the Empire.

Well, then, why did Bristol dismiss Burke? We know the ostensible reasons, because he has given them himself. One was because he voted for the relaxation of the penal laws against Roman Catholics and for the relaxation of the hide-bound commercial policy that separated England and Ireland. But I am inclined to think that the real reasons were more practical and less magnificent; I am inclined to think that the first reason why Bristol rejected Burke was that he was too negligent of his constituents, did not pay visits enough, was too long absent from them, and that through his absence his opponents were always on the spot, were constantly employed in sowing tares among his wheat. And the other reason I shall give is this, that he had no money to fight Bristol in those days, and that in those days a contest for Bristol was enormously expensive; and that while he had no money, his supporters at the first election had become impoverished owing to the unjust and foolish American War and were unable to come to his assistance. Those, at least, are the deductions I arrived at after reading the most interesting and exhaustive book on the connection of Burke with Bristol published by Mr. Weare. I confess I could hardly lay down that book until I had finished it. I have only one fault to find with it. It went to disprove and regard as without foundation a historic story of Cruger, Burke's colleague, who, when Burke sat down at the end of his great oration to the electors of Bristol, said, "Gentlemen, I say ditto to Mr. Burke." I am happy to think that time-worn anecdote is beyond reach of Mr. Weare or any other seeker after historical truth, because so good a story, when it has been current for a century, is certain to be immortal whether it be true or false.

You must remember that, as I have said, you were then the second city of the Empire and your seat was not an easy seat to win. You now get through the poll in a day. The poll then lasted from three weeks to five. All that time new electors were being admitted

APPRECIATIONS

under the guise of freemen, and as often as they were admitted they voted. Two thousand of these freemen and more were admitted during the course of the three weeks' poll when Mr. Burke was elected, and the certificates of these freemen, "copies" as they were called, were begged, borrowed, and stolen with the greatest readiness in the world. And when it was impossible to beg, borrow, steal, or manufacture any more of these certificates, one desperate course was at last resorted to, which was this—the widow or the daughter of a freeman of Bristol could confer on her second husband or on her husband the privilege of the franchise by marriage, and so these interesting ladies were dug out and discovered wherever they might exist, even in the recesses of the workhouse, and were taken to church to be married to some enterprising and ambitious politician who wished to exercise for that occasion the privilege of the franchise. It is recorded that these conscientious couples were invariably separated at the church door; the husband hurried to fulfil the new duties that had been enforced upon him by his union, and when he had done that the ceremony of divorce was gone through with equal expedition. Proceeding to the churchyard, the couple stood, each on one side of a grave, and, in allusion to the solemn words of the marriage service, they said to each other what was true in a sense, "Death does us part." Both parties went their way rejoicing. That was considered sufficient divorce of such a marriage, and I am not sure that the opinion was ill founded.

Well, for one reason or another, Burke and Bristol parted; but, after all, whether they parted or not, it is a noble episode in both their histories. That was a great period for Bristol. Four years before Burke came to this city, a lonely, starving, desperate Bristol lad of seventeen burned his manuscripts in a London garret, took poison, and made an end of himself—one of the two great poetical prodigies of the eighteenth century, Thomas Chatterton, perhaps the greatest instance on record of lonely, self-relying, self-sufficing, precocious poetical genius. Well, the short space of twenty-eight years from 1752 to

APPRECIATIONS

1780 covers the whole life of Chatterton and the whole connection of Burke with Bristol. But think how those names decorate Bristol for all time! They are, after all, the two foremost names of their time in their several departments—Chatterton, to whom Wordsworth, who was not prone to external admiration, bent in reverent homage, and Burke, of whom we need say no more at this moment. Surely we may say that Bristol was then in every sense the second city of the Empire, if not the first.

Now, let me say one word to you of Burke as apart from Bristol. It is too vast a subject for me to enter upon in any detail or as approaching any but a corner of the subject, for so wide and various are the genius and career of Burke that you might as well attempt to exhaust the character of Shakespeare in a speech of this kind as attempt to deal adequately with the genius of Burke. But what is the key to Burke's character? There is, on the face of it, some apparent complexity. Burke was an ardent reformer all his life, but ended in a frenzy of Toryism

BURKE

so violent that it transcended the Ministerial Toryism of that day. That appears inconsistent on the face of it, but it seems to me to bear no real inconsistency. The secret of Burke's character is this in my judgment—that he loved reform and hated revolution. He loved reform because he hated revolution. He hated revolution because he loved reform. He regarded revolution as the greatest possible enemy of that large, steady, persistent, moderate reform that he loved, and because by its indiscriminating violence it provoked indiscriminate reaction. And, on the other hand, he regarded reform not merely as good in itself, but as tending by its action to prevent and anticipate the horrors of revolution. Now, you know his horror of anything like Parliamentary reform. He would not touch the smallest rotten borough, he would move no hand in doing away with the slightest of those abuses which all Englishmen have long agreed to see in the Parliamentary history of his time. In my opinion, that is no real exception to the rule I have laid down, because in his judgment the balances and

APPRECIATIONS

safeguards of the Constitution hung so nicely and by so delicate an adjustment, that he had the greatest fear that if you touched them at all they would all come tumbling down together; and so when at last he did see the violence, the massacre, and the bloodshed of the French Revolution, transcending all that he had feared in a cataclysm of that kind, he burst out in a sublime frenzy of passion and denunciation.

I think to this day we feel the thrill of what he wrote then. If you remember, Sir Philip Francis wrote to complain that his description—his famous description—of Marie Antoinette and the contrast with her fallen fortunes was too florid for the exact canons of good taste. What was Burke's reply? He said, " I tell you again " that it "*did* draw tears from me and wetted my paper. These tears came again into my eyes almost as often as I looked at the description—they may again." And I think that when a genius such as this puts tears into prose, posterity may still continue to shed them. Where he failed with regard to the French Revolution was in being blinded, by his disgust at what was passing, to any appreciation of the other side of the question. He saw the horrors as we see them and as we read of them. What he did not see was that they were the outcome of a century of misgovernment, and of misrule and debauchery such as had caused a long continuance of terrible calamity. The palaces and the campaigns and the mistresses of the last two Louis had ground down the faces of the poor in France, and had made life not merely intolerable, but almost impossible to them. There is no doubt that those who suffered on the scaffold in the French Revolution were not the real causes of the Revolution, but they expiated a long series of intolerable crimes against the nation itself. And the result is that Burke passes out of history with the appearance of a reactionary to whom the reaction of his day was totally insufficient, while he passed his life as a reformer, daring and grasping enough to frighten the very souls of his admirers.

I would ask you to remember two other points in the career of Burke, two admirable

APPRECIATIONS

points to my mind. The first was his superiority to everything in the nature of private friendship and party ties when the call of duty summoned him. There was no stronger party man than Burke. He was a Whig of the Whigs. He glorified Whigs. He inspired the Whigs. He was, if I may so express myself, the prose Poet Laureate of Whiggery. And yet, without hesitation or murmur, he forsook all and followed what he believed to be the truth. He loved Charles Fox and all his other political associates. His eulogy on Charles Fox in his speech on his India Bill is perhaps the noblest tribute ever paid in eloquence by one politician to another. But he forsook them all, Charles Fox and all, to follow what he believed to be the truth. The wrench was terrible. It brought tears to the eyes of all who witnessed it. But Burke never flinched and never blenched. He went home to his lonely country home. He went home to see his son die, and all his hopes and future die with that son, and then to die in solitude and sorrow himself.

There is another point to which I would

BURKE

call your attention in regard to Burke which, as I have said, seems to me eminently creditable to him. When, in 1784, he saw himself out of office for life he did not contentedly settle down to the functions of a barren and windy opposition. He seized and grappled with vast force the huge problems of Indian administration, a topic which then in Great Britain was imperfectly understood and imperfectly appreciated, and, with a courage which may almost seem heroic, he brought the great pro-Consul of those days, Warren Hastings, to an impeachment, which was indeed unsuccessful, but which will remain always one of the most enduring monuments of his fame. I have no personal application to draw from that lesson, but I think that every earnest man must have felt in opposition the want of sincere and serious and patriotic work which may enable him to fulfil his duty to his country even when he is not able to do it in office, and that the lesson of Burke is one that has not been lost and will not be lost on our statesmen.

The last point I would call your attention

APPRECIATIONS

to in the character of Burke is this, for there is much of practical consolation to be derived by the politicians of to-day from a contemplation of the life work of Burke. Burke, though his reputation is so prodigious and is perhaps still on the rise, did not during his career perceive many of the contemporaneous symptoms of success. His speeches when they were delivered fell on deaf or heedless ears. There are two famous instances of that regret. He made a speech on Indian administration which was so wearisome and so ineffective that Dundas, who was the Minister to answer it, turned round to Pitt and they both agreed that it was not worth answering. When it came to be printed it was that famous speech on the Nabob of Arcot's debts, which Pitt and Dundas both read with a stupor of admiration and wondered as to how they could have so mistaken it when it was delivered. Another was a speech—I do not recollect at this moment which it was—but it was one which Sir Thomas Erskine, surely no mean judge of eloquence, found absolutely intolerable to listen to. I forget whether he fell asleep or went out. When it came to be published he wore out one or two copies in reading and re-reading it in a frenzy of admiration. Very well then, we see Burke's speeches were unsuccessful as speeches but not as treatises. In the next place, he rose to no high office in the State. For a few months he held one subordinate office which used to be held by men of great eminence because it had been so extremely lucrative, the office of Paymaster-General. But Burke, as the first fruits of his economic reform, practised it, which is rare, upon his own office. He cut down the emoluments and held the office with a salary which in those days was considered comparatively insignificant.

Well, then, his speeches were ineffective. He held no high office. What is the last point in which his life as regards temporary success was a failure? The last point, in my mind, is this. In none of the great objects of his earlier days did this sublime genius see any real success while he was alive. His success has followed after death, but he never lived to see it. What were his great objects?

APPRECIATIONS

Roman Catholic emancipation. He never lived to see Roman Catholic emancipation, though it has come after his death. Conciliation with America. That never came about; Ministers would not listen to it. Economical reform, the India Bill, the impeachment of Hastings, the control of the French Revolution. Is it not a consolation for us pigmies of this time, with our halting tongues and feeble weapons, to reflect that this great master of eloquence and political genius saw so little of success in his lifetime? It only exemplifies the truth of almost the last exclamation that arose from his lips in this city of Bristol, those words of which I would remind you—" What shadows we are and what shadows we pursue!" Those memorable and pathetic words which he uttered, and which sum up the life of every politician and perhaps of every man, are not less applicable to the career of Burke than to many lesser men. It is not yet a century since he passed away. We are able to realise him as he was, but in life the objects that he pursued must have seemed to him to be shadows, and they have only petrified into monuments since his death. After a long struggle between the forces of Europe and the forces of France, the French Revolution was at length controlled and subdued for a time. Roman Catholic emancipation was carried. His great policy of conciliation both to India and to Ireland was largely carried into effect, and his prospects of economical reform have been much more than realised.

And what of him? Is he a shadow? No, he is, in my opinion, the one figure of the time which is likely never to be a shadow. He brightens on the historic canvas—as the other figures fade—by his speeches, which, as I have said, were read and not listened to. He will be remembered as long as there are readers to read, when those orators on whose lips Parliaments and people hung enthralled are forgotten with the tongues that spoke and the ears that listened to them. Day by day the powerful Ministers whom he could not persuade, the great nobles whom he had to inspire and to prompt, the sublime statesmen who, forsooth, could not

APPRECIATIONS

admit him to their Cabinets, wax dimmer and dimmer, and he looms larger and stronger; for their fame rests on Bills and speeches—ephemeral Bills and ephemeral speeches—but his is built on a broader and stronger foundation, built on a high political wisdom, like some noble old castle or abbey which while it stands is a monument and beacon to man, but which often in its decay furnishes a landmark, remarkable to posterity. And so it is with the greatest pride, with the greatest pleasure, and with the most sincere admiration that I have made my pilgrimage to Bristol to-day to give my humble and faltering tribute to the great man whom you commemorate.

II

LORD CURZON has alluded to the part—the very small part—that I have played in to-day's ceremony. Small as that part was, it was distinguished by, I believe, a crucial error on a critical point. As I have been reminded by my friend the rector, I spoke of Beaconsfield, not "Beconsfield." I well knew what I was doing, and I think my friend Lord Curzon, who so ably represents this part of the world on the Conservative side of politics, will agree with me in thinking I was right. I was brought up to believe the pronunciation was "Beconsfield" until on the creation of the title of Lady Beaconsfield, and still more of Lord Beaconsfield, I was impressed by those distinguished persons with a creed, which will only leave me with my life, that the proper pronunciation was Beaconsfield, and not "Beconsfield." I can assure you it would have required more courage than I possess to address Lady Beaconsfield as Lady "Becons-

APPRECIATIONS

field," or Lord Beaconsfield as Lord " Beconsfield." I do not know how it will be fought out in this district, that conflict of pronunciation ; I only give you the historical authority on one side, and I do not know whether it will countervail local tradition on the other.

I think we have had a most interesting ceremony to-day. It has been interesting in part because of its simplicity, not because of the grandeur or of the celebrity of those who attended it, though I confess I was very glad to see a detachment of Irishmen present to do honour to the greatest of Irishmen. But I think some of us who stood in the church to-day must have felt their thoughts revert for a moment to the sublime ceremony a few weeks ago in which all that was mortal of one of the greatest of Englishmen (*Mr. Gladstone*) was enshrined in Westminster Abbey. There is a great contrast between that noble and signal procession and our little ceremony of to-day. But on the whole the little ceremony of to-day is not incongruous. It would not have taken place had Burke been buried among the great of the earth in Westminster

Abbey; and, indeed, Charles Fox proposed it, but by his will Burke absolutely forbade it. It would not have been out of place had Burke been buried in Westminster Abbey, but it seems to me to be more strictly appropriate that a man whose life was distinguished in the higher walks of thought—but not by many of the outer rewards of this world, for he was never a Cabinet Minister—should be buried, not in Westminster Abbey among those who have achieved those distinctions, but in that quiet home of his where he was seen at his best, and in the church where he worshipped among the poorer neighbours whom he loved.

There was, of course, more than one Burke. There was the Burke who has left works which will only perish with the English language, but to-day we are thinking more of the Burke as he was seen at Gregories, the farmer, the unsuccessful farmer—as all gentlemen farmers are—the man who strolled about his place, who showed with pride his pigs and his cattle and his horses and his sheep, the man for whom nothing was too small or too simple in the midst of this home. There

APPRECIATIONS

have been published in a Scotch paper quite recently extracts from the diary of a Miss Shackleton, belonging to that family of Shackletons to whom Burke had been attached all his life, which, I think, give almost the most perfect picture of Burke at Gregories I have ever read. She describes with the greatest reverence how she came to see Burke, and how he presented her to Crabbe the poet, and how Burke took her into the grounds and made his dog jump into the pond after a stick to show her how well it swam, how he showed her his stables, his granaries, and his domestic animals. And, then, how does Burke end the day? There is no light more instructive on this extraordinary man than that he ended by compounding pills for his poorer neighbours who were ill. Talk of cutting blocks with a razor! The man whose eloquence was the delight of his country, whose writings created an impulse over the world such as no political writings perhaps have ever exceeded, sat down to waste his time, as some might have thought it, in compounding rhubarb with other disagreeable adjuncts into remedies for his poorer neighbours. And as he did so he told a story which I think is worthy to be told on such an occasion as this. He said, "I am like an Irish peer whom I used to know, who was also fond of dealing out remedies to his neighbours. One day that nobleman met a funeral, and asked a poorer neighbour whose funeral it was. 'Oh, my lord,' was the reply, 'that's Tady So-and-So, the man whom your lordship cured three days ago.'"

Well, that is the side of Burke we are thinking of to-day. There has been no pompous procession to hallow this centenary, nothing in the nature of ceremony, nothing that would attract the outer eye. But I think we who have been present in the little church to-day have felt that we have taken a moment out of the world and its cares and its businesses for one higher and more sublime process of thought, that we have been enabled to enshrine in our lives a memory in thought and in prayer to-day—a memory which the world will never let die.

ROBERT BURNS

July 21st, 1896, *was the centenary of the death of Robert Burns. On the morning of that day, Lord Rosebery was at the poet's tomb, there to receive wreaths brought by deputations from all quarters of the globe. In the afternoon he delivered the first of these Appreciations in the Drill Hall at Dumfries; in the evening, the second in the St. Andrew's Hall at Glasgow.*

ROBERT BURNS

I

I COME here as a loyal burgess of Dumfries to do honour to the greatest burgess of Dumfries. You, Mr. Provost, have laid upon me a great distinction but a great burden. Your most illustrious burgess obtained privileges for his children in respect of his burgess-ship, but you impose on your youngest burgess an honour that might well break anybody's back—that of attempting to do justice in any shape or fashion to the hero of to-day's ceremony. But we citizens of Dumfries have a special claim to be considered on this day. We are surrounded by the choicest and the most sacred haunts of the poet. You have in this town the house in which he died, the "Globe," where we could

APPRECIATIONS

have wished that some phonograph had then existed which could have communicated to us some of his wise and witty and wayward talk. You have the street commemorated in M'Culloch's tragic anecdote when Burns was shunned by his former friends, and you have the paths by the Nith which are associated with some of his greatest work. You have near you the room in which the whistle was contended for, and in which, if mere legend is to be trusted, the immortal Dr. Gregory was summoned to administer his first powders to the survivors of that memorable debauch. You have the stackyard in which, lying on his back and contemplating—

> "Thou ling'ring star, with less'ning ray,
> That lov'st to greet the early morn,"

he wrote the lines "To Mary in Heaven"—perhaps the most pathetic of his poems. You have near you the walk by the river where, in his transport, he passed his wife and children without seeing them, "his brow flushed and his eyes shining" with the lustre of "Tam o' Shanter." "I wish you had but seen him," said his wife; "he was in such ecstacy that the tears were happing down his cheeks." That is why we are in Dumfries to-day. We come to honour Burns among these immortal haunts of his.

But it is not in Dumfries alone that he is commemorated to-day, for all Scotland will pay her tribute. And this, surely, is but right. Mankind owes him a general debt. But the debt of Scotland is special. For Burns exalted our race, he hallowed Scotland and the Scottish tongue. Before his time we had for a long period been scarcely recognised, we had been falling out of the recollection of the world. From the time of the union of the Crowns, and still more from the time of the legislative union, Scotland had lapsed into obscurity. Except for an occasional riot or a Jacobite rising, her existence was almost forgotten. She had, indeed, her Robertsons and her Humes writing history to general admiration, but no trace of Scottish authorship was discoverable in their works; indeed, every flavour of national idiom was carefully excluded. The Scottish dialect, as Burns called it, was in

APPRECIATIONS

danger of perishing. Burns seemed at this juncture to start to his feet and re-assert Scotland's claim to national existence; his Scottish notes rang through the world, and he thus preserved the Scottish language for ever; for mankind will never allow to die that idiom in which his songs and poems are enshrined. That is a part of Scotland's debt to Burns.

But this is much more than a Scottish demonstration; it is a collection of representatives from all quarters of the globe to own a common allegiance and a common faith. It is not only Scotsmen honouring the greatest of Scotsmen—we stretch far beyond a kingdom or a race—we are rather a sort of poetical Mohammedans gathered at a sort of poetical Mecca.

And yet we are assembled in our high enthusiasm under circumstances which are somewhat paradoxical. For with all the appearance of joy, we celebrate not a festival, but a tragedy. It is not the sunrise, but the sunset that we commemorate. It is not the birth of a new power into the world, the subtle germ of a fame that is to survive and inspire the generations of men; but it is perhaps more fitting that we celebrate the end and not the beginning. For the coming of these figures is silent; it is their disappearance that we know.. At this instant that I speak there may be born into the world the equal of a Newton or a Cæsar, but half of us would be dead before he had revealed himself. Their death is different. It may be gloomy and disastrous; it may come at a moment of shame or neglect; but by that time the man has carved his name somewhere on the Temple of Fame. There are exceptions, of course; cases where the end comes before the slightest, or any but the slightest, recognition —Chatterton choking in his garret, hunger of body and soul all unsatisfied; Millet selling his pictures for a song; nay, Shakespeare himself. But, as a rule, death in the case of genius closes the first act of a public drama; criticism and analysis may then begin their unbiased work free from jealousy or friendship or personal consideration for the living. Then comes the third act, if third act there be.

No, it is a death, not a birth, that we cele-

APPRECIATIONS

brate. This day a century ago, in poverty, delirium, and distress, there was passing the soul of Robert Burns. To him death comes in clouds and darkness, the end of a long agony of body and soul; he is harassed with debt, his bodily constitution is ruined, his spirit is broken, his wife is daily expecting her confinement. He has lost almost all that rendered his life happy—much of friendship, credit, and esteem. Some score years before, one of the most charming of English writers, as he lay dying, was asked if his mind was at ease, and with his last breath Oliver Goldsmith owned that it was not. So it was with Robert Burns. His delirium dwelt on the horrors of a jail; he uttered curses on the tradesman who was pursuing him for debt. "What business," said he to his physician in a moment of consciousness, "what business has a physician to waste his time upon me; I am a poor pigeon not worth plucking. Alas! I have not feathers enough to carry me to my grave." For a year or more his health had been failing. He had a poet's body as well as a poet's mind; nervous, feverish, impressionable; and his constitution, which, it nursed and regulated, might have carried him to the limit of life, was unequal to the storm and stress of dissipation and a preying mind. In the previous autumn he had been seized with a rheumatic attack; his digestion had given way; he was sunk in melancholy and gloom. In his last April he wrote to his friend Thomson, "By Babel's streams, &c. Almost ever since I wrote you last, I have only known existence by the pressure of the heavy hand of Sickness, and have counted time by the repercussions of pain! Rheumatism, cold, and fever, have formed, to me, a terrible Trinity in Unity, which makes me close my eyes in misery, and open them without hope." It was sought to revive him by sea bathing, and he went to stay at Brow Well. There he remained three weeks, but was under no delusion as to his state. "Well, madam," he said to Mrs. Riddell on arriving, "have you any commands for the other world?" He sat that evening with his old friend, and spoke manfully of his approaching death, of the fate of his children, and his fame; sometimes indulging in bittersweet pleasantry, but never losing the consciousness of his condition. In three weeks he wearied of the fruitless hunt for health, and he returned home to die. He was only just in time. When he re-entered his home on the 18th he could no longer stand; he was soon delirious; in three days he was dead. "On the fourth day," we are told, "when his attendant held a cordial to his lips, he swallowed it eagerly, rose almost wholly up, spread out his hands, sprang forward nigh the whole length of the bed, fell on his face, and expired."

I suppose there are many who can read the account of these last months with composure. They are more fortunate than I. There is nothing much more melancholy in all biography. The brilliant poet, the delight of all society, from the highest to the lowest, sits brooding in silence over the drama of his spent life; the early innocent home, the plough and the savour of fresh-turned earth; the silent communion with Nature and his own heart, the brief hour of splendour, the dark hour of neglect, the mad struggle for forgetfulness, the bitterness of vanished homage, the gnawing doubt of fame, the distressful future of his wife and children—an endless witch-dance of thought without clue or remedy, all perplexing, all soon to end while he is yet young, as men reckon youth; though none know so well as he that his youth is gone, his race is run, his message is delivered.

His death revived the flagging interest and pride that had been felt for him. As usual, men began to realise what they had lost when it was too late. When it was known that he was dying the townspeople had shown anxiety and distress. They recalled his fame and forgot his fall. One man was heard to ask, with a touch of quaint simplicity, "Who do you think will be our poet now?" The district set itself to prepare a public funeral for the poet who died penniless among them. A vast concourse followed him to his grave. The awkward squad, as he had foreseen and deprecated, fired volleys over his coffin. The streets were lined with soldiers, among them one who, within sixteen years, was to be

APPRECIATIONS

Prime Minister. And while the procession wended its gloomy way, as if no element of tragedy were to be wanting, his widow's hour of travail arrived and she gave birth to the hapless child that had caused the father so much misgiving. In this place and on this day it all seems present to us—the house of anguish, the thronged churchyard, the weeping neighbours. We feel ourselves part of the mourning crowd. We hear those dropping volleys and that muffled drum; we bow our heads as the coffin passes, and acknowledge with tears the inevitable doom. Pass, heavy hearse, with thy weary freight of shattered hopes and exhausted frame; pass, with thy simple pomp of fatherless bairns and sad moralising friends; pass, with the sting of death to the victory of the grave; pass, with the perishable, and leave us the eternal.

It is rare to be fortunate in life; it is infinitely rarer to be fortunate in death. "Happy in the occasion of his death," as Tacitus said of Agricola, is not a common epitaph. It is comparatively easy to know how to live, but it is beyond all option and choice to compass the more difficult art of knowing when and how to die. We can generally by looking back choose a moment in a man's life when he had been fortunate had he dropped down dead. And so the question arises naturally to-day, was Burns fortunate in his death—that death which we commemorate? There can, I fancy, be only one answer; it was well that he died when he did; it might even have been better for himself had he died a little earlier. The terrible letters that he wrote two years before to Mrs. Riddell and Mr. Cunningham betoken a spirit mortally wounded. In those last two years the cloud settles, never to be lifted. "My constitution and frame were *ab origine* blasted with a deep incurable taint of hypochondria which poisons my existence." He found perhaps some pleasure in the composition of his songs, some occasional relief in the society of boon companions; but the world was fading before him.

There is an awful expression in Scotland which one never hears without a pang—"So-and-so is *done*," meaning that he is physically worn out. Burns was "done." He was struggling on like a wounded deer to his death. He had often faced the end, and not unwillingly. "Can it be possible," he once wrote to Mrs. Dunlop, " that when I resign this frail, feverish being, I shall still find myself in conscious existence? When the last gasp of agony has announced that I am no more to those that know me, and the few who loved me; when the cold, stiffened, unconscious, ghastly corse is resigned into the earth, to be the prey of unsightly reptiles, and to become in time a trodden clod, shall I yet be warm in life, seeing and seen, enjoying and enjoyed?" Surely that reads as if he foresaw this day and would fain be with us—as indeed he may be. Twelve years before he had faced death in a less morbid spirit:

"Why [he asked] am I loth to leave this earthly scene?
 Have I so found it full of pleasing charms—
Some drops of joy with draughts of ill between—
 Some gleams of sunshine 'mid renewing storms?"

He had, perhaps, never enjoyed life so much as is supposed, though he had turned to it a brave, cheerful, unflinching face, and the last years had been years of misery. "God have mercy on me," he wrote years before the end, "a poor damned, incautious, duped, unfortunate fool! The sport, the miserable victim of rebellious pride, hypochondriac imagination, agonising sensibility, and bedlam passions." There was truth in this outburst. At any rate, his most devoted friends—and to be an admirer of Burns is to be his friend—may wish that he had not lived to write the letter to Mr. Clark, piteously pleading that a harmless toast may not be visited hardly upon him; or that to Mrs. Riddell, beginning: "I write you from the regions of Hell, amid the horrors of the damned"; or to be harried by his official superiors as a political suspect; shunned by his fashionable friends for the same reason; wandering like a neglected ghost in Dumfries, avoided and ignored. "That's all over now, my young friend," he said, speaking of his reign in society, "and werena my heart licht I wad dee." All this was in 1794. Had he died before then, it might have been happier for himself, and we

APPRECIATIONS

should have lost some parts of his life which we would rather forget ; but posterity could not have spared him ; we could not have lost the exquisite songs which we owe to those years ; but, above all, the supreme creed and comfort which he bequeathed to the world—

"A man's a man for a' that,"

would have remained undelivered.

One may, perhaps, go further and say that poets—or those whom the gods love—should die young. This is a hard saying, but it will not greatly affect the bills of mortality. And it applies only to poets of the first rank; while even here it has its exceptions, and illustrious exceptions they are. But surely the best poetry is produced before middle age, before the morning and its illusions have faded, before the heaviness of noon and the baleful cool of evening. Few men, too, can bear the strain of a poet's temperament through many years. At any rate, we may feel sure of this, that Burns had produced his best, that he would never again have produced a "Tam o' Shanter," or a "Cottar's Saturday

Night," or a "Jolly Beggars"; and that long before his death, though he could still write lines affluent with tenderness and grace, " the hand of pain and sorrow and care," to use his own words, " had lain heavy upon " him.

And this leads to another point. To-day is not merely the melancholy anniversary of death, but the rich and incomparable fulfilment of prophecy. For this is the moment to which Burns looked when he said to his wife : "Don't be afraid; I'll be more respected a hundred years after I am dead than I am at present ! " To-day the hundred years are completed, and we can judge of the prediction. On that point we must all be unanimous. Burns had honour in his lifetime, but his fame has rolled like a snowball since his death, and it rolls on. There is, indeed, no parallel to it in the world ; it sets the calculations of compound interest at defiance. He is not merely the watchword of a nation that carries and implants Burns-worship all over the globe as birds carry seeds, but he has become the champion and patron saint of Democracy. He bears the banner of

APPRECIATIONS

the essential equality of man. His birthday is celebrated—137 years after its occurrence—more universally than that of any human being. He reigns over a greater dominion than any empire that the world has ever seen. Nor does the ardour of his devotees decrease. Ayr and Ellisland, Mauchline and Dumfries, are the shrines of countless pilgrims. Burns statues are a hardy annual. The production of Burns manuscripts was a lucrative branch of industry until it was checked by untimely intervention. The editions of Burns are as the sands of the sea. No canonised name in the calendar excites so blind and enthusiastic a worship. Whatever Burns may have contemplated in his prediction, whatever dream he may have fondled in the wildest moments of elation, must have fallen utterly short of the reality. And it is all spontaneous. There is no puff, no advertisement, no manipulation. Intellectual cosmetics of that kind are frail and fugitive; they rarely survive their subject; they would not have availed here. Nor was there any glamour attached to the poet; rather the reverse. He has stood by himself; he has grown by himself. It is himself and no other that we honour.

But what had Burns in his mind when he made this prediction? It might be whimsically urged that he was conscious that the world had not yet seen his masterpiece, for the "Jolly Beggars" was not published till some time after his death. But that would not be sufficient, for he had probably forgotten its existence. Nor do I think he spoke at haphazard. What were perhaps present to his mind were the fickleness of his contemporaries towards him, his conviction of the essential splendour of his work, the consciousness that the incidents of his later years had unjustly obscured him, and that his true figure would be perceived as these fell away into forgetfulness or were measured at their true value. If so, he was right in his judgment, for his true life began with his death; with the body passed all that was gross and impure; the clear spirit stood revealed; and soared at once to its accepted place among the fixed stars, in the firmament of the rare immortals.

II

WE are here to-day to celebrate Burns. What the direct connection of Burns with Glasgow may be I am not exactly sure; but, at any rate, I am confident of this, that in the great metropolis of the West there is a clear claim that we should celebrate the genius of Robert Burns. I have celebrated it already elsewhere. I cannot, perhaps, deny that the day has been a day of labour, but it has been a labour of love. It is, and it must be, a source of joy and pride to us to see our champion Scotsman receive the honour and admiration and affection of humanity; to see, as I have seen this morning, the long processions bringing homage and tribute to the conquering dead. But these have only been signs and symptoms of the world-wide passion of reverence and devotion. That generous and immortal soul pervades the universe to-day. In the humming city and in the crowd of man; in the backwood and

ROBERT BURNS

in the swamp; where the sentinel paces the bleak frontier, and where the sailor smokes his evening pipe; and above all, where the farmer and his men pursue their summer toil, whether under the Stars and Stripes or under the Union Jack—the thought and sympathy of men are directed to Robert Burns.

I have sometimes asked myself, if a rollcall of fame were read over at the beginning of every century, how many men of eminence would answer a second time to their names. But of our poet there is no doubt or question. The *adsum* of Burns rings out clear and unchallenged. There are few before him on the list, and we cannot now conceive a list without him. He towers high, and yet he lived in an age when the average was sublime.

It sometimes seems to me as if the whole eighteenth century was a constant preparation for, a constant working up to, the great drama of the revolution which closed it. The scenery is all complete when the time arrives—the dark volcanic country; the hungry desperate people; the firefly nobles; the concentrated splendour of the Court—in the midst, in her

APPRECIATIONS

place as heroine, the dazzling Queen. And during long previous years brooding nature had been producing not merely the immediate actors, but figures worthy of the scene. What a glittering procession it is! We can only mark some of the principal figures. Burke leads the way; then come Fox and Goethe; Nelson and Mozart; Schiller, Pitt, and Burns; Wellington and Napoleon. And among these Titans, Burns is a conspicuous figure, the figure which appeals most of all to the imagination and affection of mankind. Napoleon looms larger to the imagination, but on the affection he has no hold. It is in the combination of the two powers that Burns is supreme.

What is his secret? We are always discussing him and endeavouring to find it out. Perhaps, like the latent virtue of some medicinal baths, it may never be satisfactorily explained. But, at any rate, let us discuss him again. That is, I presume, our object to-night. What pleasanter or more familiar occupation can there be for Scotsmen? But the Scotsmen who enjoy it have generally perhaps more time than I. Pardon then the imperfections of my speech, for I speak of a subject which no one can altogether compass, and which a busy man has perhaps no right to attempt.

The clue to Burns's extraordinary hold on mankind is possibly a complicated one; it has, perhaps, many developments. If so, we have not time to consider it to-night. But I personally believe the causes are, like most great causes, simple; though it might take long to point out all the ways in which they operate. The secret, as it seems to me, lies in two words—inspiration and sympathy. But if I wished to prove my contention, I should go on quoting from his poems all night, and his admirers would still declare that I had omitted the best passages. I know that profuse quotation is a familiar form of a Burns speech; but I am afraid to begin lest I should not end, and I am sure that I should not satisfy. I must proceed then in a more summary way.

Now, there seem to me to be two great natural forces in British literature. I use

APPRECIATIONS

the safe adjective of British, and your applause shows me that I was right to do so. I use it partly because hardly any of Burns's poetry is strictly English; partly because he hated, and was perhaps the first to protest against, the use of the word English as including Scottish. Well, I say there are in that literature two great forces of which the power seems sheer inspiration and nothing else—Shakespeare and Burns. This is not the place or the time to speak of that miracle called Shakespeare, but one must say a word of the miracle called Burns.

Try and reconstruct Burns as he was. A peasant, born in a cottage that no sanitary inspector in these days would tolerate for a moment; struggling with desperate effort against pauperism, almost in vain; snatching at scraps of learning in the intervals of toil, as it were with his teeth; a heavy silent lad, proud of his ploughing. All of a sudden, without preface or warning, he breaks out into exquisite song, like a nightingale from the brushwood, and continues singing as sweetly — with nightingale pauses — till he dies. A nightingale sings because he cannot help it; he can only sing exquisitely, because he knows no other. So it was with Burns. What is this but inspiration? One can no more measure or reason about it than measure or reason about Niagara.

Under the limitations which I have imposed on myself to-night, we must take for granted the incomparable excellence of his poetry. But I must ask you to remember that the poetry is only a fragment of Burns. Amazing as it may seem, all contemporary testimony is unanimous that the man was far more wonderful than his works. " It will be an injustice done to Burns's reputation," writes an accomplished lady, who might well have judged him harshly, " in the records of literature, not only as respects future generations and foreign countries, but even with his nativeScotland and some of his contemporaries, that he is generally talked of and considered with reference to his poetical talents *only*. . . . Poetry," she continues, " (I appeal to all who had the advantage of personal acquaintance with him) was actually not his *forte*. . . . None certainly ever out-shone Burns in the charms —the sorcery I would almost call it—of fascinating conversation, the spontaneous eloquence of social argument, or the unstudied poignancy of brilliant repartee." And she goes on to describe the almost superhuman fascination of his voice and of his eyes, those balls of black fire which electrified all on whom they rested.

It seems strange to be told that it would be an injustice to judge Burns by his poetry alone; but as to the magnetism of his presence and conversation there is only one verdict. "No man's conversation ever carried me so completely off my feet," said the Duchess of Gordon—the friend of Pitt and of the London wits, the queen of Scottish society. Dugald Stewart says that "all the faculties of Burns's mind were, so far as I could judge, equally vigorous; and his predilection for poetry was rather the result of his own enthusiastic and impassioned temper than of a genius exclusively adapted to that species of composition. From his conversation I should have pronounced him to be fitted to excel in whatever walk of ambition he had chosen to exert his abilities." And of his prose compositions the same severe judge speaks thus : "Their great and various excellences render some of them scarcely less objects of wonder than his poetical performances. The late Dr. Robertson used to say that, considering his education, the former seemed to him the more extraordinary of the two." "I think Burns," said Principal Robertson to a friend, " was one of the most extraordinary men I ever met with. His poetry surprised me very much, his prose surprised me still more, and his conversation surprised me more than both his poetry and prose." We are told, too, that " he felt a strong call towards oratory, and all who heard him speak—and some of them were excellent judges — admitted his wonderful quickness of apprehension and readiness of eloquence." All this seems to me marvellous. It surely ratifies the claim of inspiration without the necessity of quoting a line of his poetry.

APPRECIATIONS

I pass then to his sympathy. If his talents were universal, his sympathy was not less so. His tenderness was not a mere selfish tenderness for his own family, for he loved all mankind except the cruel and the base. Nay, we may go further and say that he placed all creation, especially the suffering and despised part of it, under his protection. The oppressor in every shape, even in the comparatively innocent embodiment of the factor and the sportsman, he regarded with direct and personal hostility. But above all he saw the charm of the home; he recognised it as the basis of all society, he honoured it in its humblest form, for he knew, as few know, how unpretentiously, but how sincerely, the family in the cottage is welded by mutual love and esteem. "I recollect once," said Dugald Stewart, speaking of Burns, " he told me, when I was admiring a distant prospect in one of our morning walks, that the sight of so many smoking cottages gave a pleasure to his mind which none could understand who had not witnessed, like himself, the happiness and the worth which they contained." He dwells repeatedly on the primary sacredness of the home and the family, the responsibility of fatherhood and marriage. "Have not I," he once wrote to Lord Mar, "a more precious stake in my country's welfare than the richest dukedom in it? I have a large family of children, and the probability of more." The lines in which he tells his faith are not less memorable than the stately stanzas in which Gray sings the "short and simple annals of the poor." I must quote them again, often quoted as they are :

> "To make a happy fireside clime
> To weans and wife,
> That's the true pathos and sublime
> Of human life."

His verses, then, go straight to the heart of every home ; they appeal to every father and mother. But that is only the beginning, perhaps the foundation, of his sympathy. There is something for everybody in Burns. He has a heart even for vermin ; he has pity even for the arch-enemy of mankind. And his universality makes his poems a treasure-house in which all may find what they want. Every wayfarer in the journey of life may pluck strength and courage from it as he passes. The sore, the weary, the wounded, will all find something to heal and soothe. For this great master is the universal Samaritan. Where the priest and the Levite may have passed by in vain, this eternal heart will still afford a resource. But he is not only for the sick in spirit. The friend, the lover, the patriot, will all find their choicest refreshment in Burns. His touch is everywhere, and it is everywhere the touch of genius. Nothing comes amiss to him. What was said of the debating power of his eminent contemporary, Dundas, may be said of his poetry: "He went out in all weathers." And it may be added that all weathers suited him; that he always brought back something precious, something we cherish, something that cannot die.

He is, then, I think, the universal friend in an unique sense. But he was, poetically speaking, the special friend of Scotland, in a sense which recalls a profound remark of another eminent Scotsman, I mean Fletcher of Saltoun. In an account of a conversation between Lord Cromarty, Sir Edward Seymour, Sir Christopher Musgrave, and himself, Fletcher writes: "I said I knew a very wise man, so much of Sir Christopher's sentiment that he believed if a man were permitted to make all the ballads, he need not care who should make the laws of a nation." This may be rudely paraphrased, that it is more important to make the songs of a nation than to frame its laws, and this again may be interpreted to mean that in the days of Fletcher, at any rate, as in the days of Burns, it is the familiar songs of a people that mould their thoughts, their manners, and their morals. If this be true, can we exaggerate the debt that we Scotsmen owe to Burns? He has bequeathed to his country the most exquisite casket of songs in the world; primarily to his country, though others cannot be denied their share. I will give only one example, but that is a signal one. From distant Roumania the Queen of that country wrote to Dumfries to-day that she has no copy of

APPRECIATIONS

Burns with her, but that she knows his songs by heart.

We must remember, too, that there is more than this to be said. Many of Burns's songs were already in existence in the lips and minds of the people—rough and coarse and obscene. Our benefactor takes them, and with a touch of inspired alchemy transmutes them and leaves them pure gold. He loved the old catches and the old tunes, and into these gracious moulds he poured his exquisite gifts of thought and expression. But for him, those ancient airs, often wedded to words which no decent man could recite, would have perished from that corruption if not from neglect. He rescued them for us by his songs, and in doing so he hallowed the life and sweetened the breath of Scotland.

I have also used the words patriot and lover. These draw me to different lines of thought. The word "patriot" leads me to the political side of Burns. There is no doubt that he was suspected of being a politician; and he is even said to have sometimes wished to enter Parliament. That was perhaps an excusable aberration, and my old friend Professor Masson has, I think, surmised that had he lived he might have been a great Liberal pressman. My frail thought shall not dally with such surmise, but it conducts us naturally to the subject of Burns's politics. From his sympathy for his own class, from his indignation against nobles like the Duke of Queensberry, and from the toasts that cost him so dear, it might be considered easy to infer his political opinions. But Burns should not be claimed for any party. A poet, be it remembered, is never a politician, and a politician is never a poet— that is to say, a politician is never so fortunate as to be a poet, and a poet is so fortunate as never to be a politician. I do not say that the line of demarcation is never passed—a politician may have risen for a moment, or a poet may have descended ; but where there is any confusion between the two callings, it is generally because the poet thinks he discerns, or the politician thinks he needs, something higher than politics. Burns's politics were entirely governed by his imagination. He

APPRECIATIONS

was at once a Jacobite and a Jacobin. He had the sad sympathy which most of us have felt for the hapless house of Stuart, without the least wish to be governed by it. He had much the same sort of abstract sympathy with the French Revolution, when it was setting all Europe to rights ; but he was prepared to lay down his life to prevent its putting this island to rights. And then came his official superiors of the Excise, who, notwithstanding Mr. Pitt's admiration of his poetry, snuffed out his politics without remorse.

The name of Pitt leads me to add that Burns had some sort of relation with three Prime Ministers. Colonel Jenkinson, of the Cinque Ports Fencible Cavalry—afterwards Minister for fifteen years under the title of Liverpool—was on duty at Burns's funeral, though we are told—the good man—that he disapproved of the poet, and declined to make his acquaintance. Pitt, again, passed on Burns one of his rare and competent literary judgments, so eulogistic, indeed, that one wonders that a powerful Minister could have allowed one whom he admired so much to exist on an exciseman's pay when well, and an exciseman's half-pay when dying. And from Addington, another Prime Minister, Burns elicited a sonnet, which, in the Academy of Lagado, would surely have been held a signal triumph of the art of extracting sunshine from cucumbers.

So much for politics in the party sense. "A man's a man for a' that" is not politics—it is the assertion of the rights of humanity in a sense far wider than politics. It erects all mankind; it is the charter of its self-respect. It binds, it heals, it revives, it invigorates; it sets the bruised and broken on their legs, it refreshes the stricken soul, it is the salve and tonic of character; it cannot be narrowed into politics. Burns's politics are indeed nothing but the occasional overflow of his human sympathy into past history and current events.

And now, having discussed the two trains of thought suggested by the words "friend" and "patriot," I come to the more dangerous word "lover." There is an eternal controversy which, it appears, no didactic oil will

APPRECIATIONS

ever assuage, as to Burns's private life and morality. Some maintain that these have nothing to do with his poems; some maintain that his life must be read into his works, and here again some think that his life damns his poems, while others aver that his poems cannot be fully appreciated without his life. Another school thinks that his vices have been exaggerated, while their opponents scarcely think such exaggeration possible. It is impossible to avoid taking a side. I walk on the ashes, knowing the fire beneath, and unable to avoid it, for the topic is inevitable. I must confess myself, then, one of those who think that the life of Burns doubles the interest of his poems, and I doubt whether the failings of his life have been much exaggerated, for contemporary testimony on that point is strong; though a high authority, Mr. Wallace, has recently taken the other side with much power and point.

But the life of Burns, which I love to read with his poems, does not consist in his vices; they lie outside it. It is a life of work, and truth, and tenderness. And though, like all lives, it has its light and shade, remember that we know it all, the worst as well as the best. His was a soul bathed in crystal, he hurried to avow everything. There was no reticence in him. The only obscure passage in his life is the love passage with Highland Mary, and as to that he was silent not from shame, but because it was a sealed and sacred episode. "What a flattering idea," he once wrote, "is a world to come! There shall I with speechless agony of rapture again recognise my lost, my ever dear Mary! whose bosom was fraught with truth, honour, constancy, and love." He had, as the French say, the defects of his qualities. His imagination was a supreme and celestial gift. But his imagination often led him wrong, and never more than with women. The chivalry that made Don Quixote see the heroic in all the common events of life made Burns (as his brother tells us) see a goddess in every girl that he approached. Hence many love affairs, and some guilty ones; but even these must be judged with reference to time and circumstance. This much is certain, that had he been devoid of

APPRECIATIONS

genius they would not have attracted attention. It is Burns's pedestal that affords a target. And why, one may ask, is not the same measure meted out to Burns as to others? The bastards of great captains and statesmen and princes are treated as historical and ornamental incidents. They strut the scene of Shakespeare, and ruff it with the best. It is for the unlawful children of Burns, though he and his wife cherished them as if born in wedlock, that the vials of wrath are reserved. Take two brilliant figures, both of royal ancestry, who were alive during Burns's life. We occupy ourselves endlessly and severely with the lapses of Burns. We heave an elegant sigh over the kindred frailties of Charles James Fox and Charles Edward Stuart.

Again, it is quite clear that, though exceptionally sober in his earlier years, he drank too much in later life. But this, it must be remembered, was but an occasional condescendence to the vice and habit of the age. The gentry who pressed him to their houses, and who were all convivial, have much to answer for. His admirers who thronged to see him, and who could only conveniently sit with him in a tavern, are also responsible for this habit, so perilously attractive to men of genius. From the decorous Addison and the brilliant Bolingbroke onward, the eighteenth century records hard drinking as the common incident of intellectual eminence. To a man who had shone supreme in the most glowing society, and who was now an exciseman in a country town, with a home that cannot have been very exhilarating, and with a nervous system highly strung, the temptation of the warm tavern, and the admiring circle there, may well have been almost irresistible. Some attempt to say that his intemperance was exaggerated. I neither affirm nor deny. It was not as a sot he drank; that no one insinuated; if he succumbed it was to good fellowship.

Remember, I do not seek to palliate or excuse, and, indeed, none will be turned to dissipation by Burns's example; he paid too dearly for it. But I will say this, that it all seems infinitely little, infinitely remote. Why

APPRECIATIONS

do we strain, at this distance, to discern this dim spot on the poet's mantle? Shakespeare and Ben Jonson took their cool tankard at the Mermaid; we cannot afford, in the strictest view of literary responsibility, to quarrel with them for that. When we consider Pitt and Goethe we do not concentrate our vision on Pitt's bottles of port or Goethe's bottles of Moselle. Then why, we ask, is there such a chasm between the Mermaid and the Globe, and why are the vintages of Wimbledon and Weimar so much more innocent than the simple punch-bowl of Inverary marble and its contents?

I should like to go a step further and affirm that we have something to be grateful for even in the weaknesses of men like Burns. Mankind is helped in its progress almost as much by the study of imperfection as by the contemplation of perfection. Had we nothing before us in our futile and halting lives but saints and the ideal we might well fail altogether. We grope blindly along the catacombs of the world, we climb the dark ladder of life, we feel our way to futurity, but we can scarcely see an inch around or before us. We stumble and falter and fall, our hands and knees are bruised and sore, and we look up for light and guidance. Could we see nothing but distant unapproachable impeccability, we might well sink prostrate in the hopelessness of emulation and the weariness of despair. Is it not then, when all seems blank and lightless and lifeless, when strength and courage flag, and when perfection seems as remote as a star, is it not then that imperfection helps us? When we see that the greatest and choicest images of God have had their weaknesses like ours, their temptations, their hours of darkness, their bloody sweat, are we not encouraged by their lapses and catastrophes to find energy for one more effort, one more struggle? Where they failed we feel it a less dishonour to fail; their errors and sorrows make, as it were, an easier ascent from infinite imperfection to infinite perfection. Man after all is not ripened by virtue alone. Were it so this world were a paradise of angels. No! Like the growth of the earth, he is the fruit of all the seasons; the accident of a thousand accidents, a living mystery, moving through the seen to the unseen. He is sown in dishonour; he is matured under all the varieties of heat and cold; in mist and wrath, in snow and vapours, in the melancholy of autumn, in the torpor of winter, as well as in the rapture and fragrance of summer, or the balmy affluence of the spring—its breath, its sunshine, its dew. And at the end he is reaped—the product, not of one climate, but of all; not of good alone, but of evil; not of joy alone, but of sorrow—perhaps mellowed and ripened, perhaps stricken and withered and sour. How, then, shall we judge any one? How, at any rate, shall we judge a giant, great in gifts and great in temptation; great in strength and great in weakness? Let us glory in his strength and be comforted in his weakness. And when we thank heaven for the inestimable gift of Burns, we do not need to remember wherein he was imperfect, we cannot bring ourselves to regret that he was made of the same clay as ourselves.

WALLACE

The Sixth Centenary of the Battle of Stirling was celebrated at Stirling on September 13th, 1897. In the afternoon there was an open-air demonstration, with speeches at the National Wallace Monument on Abbey Craig. At night Provost Kinross and the Custodiers of the Monument gave a banquet at the Public Hall, at which Lord Rosebery proposed the toast of "The immortal memory of Sir William Wallace."

WALLACE

I WOULD gladly have exchanged toasts with either of the distinguished friends who have preceded me on the list, more especially since I am expected not so much to propose a toast as to deliver a historical address. I confess that I have come here more or less prepared, or rather more or less unprepared, to propose a toast. But if I had known that I was expected to deliver a historical address I should have claimed to exchange with one at least of my friends. I do not care which of the Balfours I had been chosen to fill the place of, whether it had been my noble friend on my left (*Lord Balfour of Burleigh*) or my right hon. friend on my right (*Mr. J. B. Balfour*) ; but I would rather have responded for any toast or proposed any toast than come here under the hypothesis that I was to deliver a historical address on so thorny a subject as Sir William Wallace. I humbly submit that even to propose his memory is a very perilous task.

There are, I think, two classes of my fellow countrymen who would gladly be in the position in which I find myself. One is the class of minute archæological historians, who would find a savage, an almost devilish, delight in winnowing the true from the false in the legends that surround Sir William Wallace, and in distinguishing all that is legendary from the few golden facts which remain. But I think that you will agree with me this would not be the occasion for such a discourse, and, were it the occasion, I am not the man. After all, these points are not always of very first-rate importance. There is, however, one to which I will allude. It is sometimes, I believe, the subject of controversy as to whether Wallace was a Scotsman at all. I regard that as a point of the most infinitesimal importance. It may be a subject of interest to many to know what is the birthplace or the district in which a person is brought up when that person has achieved a certain eminence; but there are greater figures than these, who embody and absorb a nation and whom a nation has absorbed and embodied, but whose exact place of birth is a matter of no importance at all. We all know that Catherine II. of Russia was a German princess. We all know that the first Napoleon was of Italian origin and born in Corsica. But I do not suppose there is anybody who has read a page of history who will deny that Catherine is one of the greatest of Russians and that Napoleon is incomparably the greatest of Frenchmen.

Then there is another class who would have rejoiced to fill my place, but I am not sure either that they would have been the right persons—I mean the class of passionate and indiscriminating patriots to whom everything, true or false, connected with the memory of a national hero is dear, and who, without the faintest effort or stress of deglutition, can swallow every legend and every tradition that is associated with their favourite hero. Sir, those patriots would soar into

APPRECIATIONS

heights to which I cannot aspire, and I venture to think that in so soaring they are not always performing a wise or patriotic task; because I firmly believe that the stronger, and the broader, and the safer the base for your enthusiasm the better it is for that enthusiasm; and that exaggeration, in matters of enthusiasm, is apt to lead to ridicule and to reaction.

The authentic and received facts about Sir William Wallace are, indeed, extremely few, but this, in my judgment—and I hope you will accept that judgment—so far from diminishing the merit of that great man, seems to me a conclusive proof of his greatness. That with so small a substratum of historical events he should have left so great an impression upon his countrymen would in itself prove him to be one of the greatest of Scotsmen. But the facts, whether few or many, are thunderbolts in themselves. The first is his own appearance—his magical, portentous, meteorical, providential appearance in the midst of the ruin, the suffering, and the disaster of his country. Fordun, the historian, describes it in words which are better

WALLACE

than any I can use. "The same year," says Fordun, "William Wallace lifted up his head from his den, as it were." He came, I say, as a portent or meteor in the distracted condition of Scotland. The next salient fact in his career, is this—the great battle of Stirling, which we commemorate to-day, in which he repulsed with very inadequate means the overwhelming forces of the English. Then there comes his appointment as guardian or protector of Scotland. Then there comes the battle of Falkirk, which might, and we believe would, have been a victory had not the desertion, at a critical moment, of his cavalry, led by the Scottish nobles, who were associated with him, decided the fortune of the day. That is the only connection I can find for my noble friend Lord Balfour between Wallace and the House of Lords—and I think, under the circumstances, he was wise to avoid the subject. Then, disgusted with this treachery, Wallace resigns the guardianship and the government of Scotland. The words in which Fordun records his resignation are so significant that I will venture once more to quote that historian: " But after the aforesaid victory which was vouchsafed to the enemy through the treachery of Scots, the aforesaid William Wallace, perceiving, by this and other strong proofs, the glaring wickedness of the Comyns and their abettors, chose rather to serve with the crowd than to be set over them, to their ruin and the grievous wasting of the people; so not long after the battle of Falkirk, at the Water of Forth, he of his own accord resigned the office or charge which he held of guardian." Then he disappears into France for a few years. Then he comes back into Scotland, is captured, as some say, by treachery again, and is condemned to a cruel and shameful death in London, almost exactly eight years after the crowning victory of Stirling Bridge. These are the great and salient facts of Wallace's history, and they are so few that we may well wonder how so short a record has so powerfully impressed the imaginations of mankind.

But I think the causes are not very far to seek. The first I will mention is the least of them all. It is his biographer, Blind

Harry. I believe that Blind Harry's record is now generally condemned as apocryphal and legendary; but this decision of historical criticism comes too late to overtake the impression made upon mankind. Dr. Moir, his most recent editor, says of his History that it has passed through more editions than any other Scottish book before the times of Burns and of Scott—that it was the book, next to the Bible, most frequently found in Scottish households. Burns tells us that it poured a Scottish prejudice into his veins " which will boil there till the floodgates of life shut in eternal rest," and we know in his famous lyric how that impression was reproduced. Well, no one can, I think, exaggerate the effect of such a leaven as this upon our national life. Nothing, however destructive the criticism may be, can now obliterate the impression that it has caused. A hero may die unknown and unhonoured without a biographer. Many a hero does. And therefore the memory of Wallace, great in itself as it may be, does owe a considerable debt to the imaginative and vivacious chronicler of his deeds.

APPRECIATIONS

Well, the next cause to which I would assign the impression left by Wallace is this, that the cause he headed was a great popular cause. The natural leaders of the people had either failed them, or betrayed them, or forsaken them, and so fierce were the internal divisions that raged between the leaders of the Scottish people, that one of them, Sir Richard Lundin, went over to Edward, justifying his defection by the declaration, " I will remain no longer of a party that is at variance with itself." The people turned to the new man with a new hope and with new expectation ; and as he was deserted by the aristocracy and the priesthood, he became essentially the man of the people.

But there is a simpler reason than either of those which I have given why the memory of Wallace is so green among us. It is simply this—that he was a great man. He was one of those men who appear with a single stamp of their foot to leave their impress upon history as the footprint which startled Crusoe remains eternal on the world of romance. No man but a great man could have so roused and concentrated the people of Scotland; no man but a great man could have been the centre round which the legends of Blind Harry clustered and remain. Why, what does Lord Hailes say of Henry II.? We may adopt the same words, I think, in speaking of Wallace. He says—but with a different intention—"I am afraid that no Scotsman can draw his character with impartiality." But, if any Scotsman can draw the character of Wallace with impartiality it is our historian, John Hill Burton. John Hill Burton had many merits as a historian. He was not enthusiastic, he was not even dramatic enough for most of us, but when we cite him as a witness he has this incalculable advantage, that he is perfectly cold and dispassionate. What does he say of Wallace after examining minutely into his career? He says—" He was a man of vast political and military genius." Well, I suspect that we need look very little into the career of Wallace to justify that encomium. That he should have leaped into the supreme power in Scotland at a single bound, that he should have overthrown

APPRECIATIONS

the overwhelming armaments of England with the very imperfect means at his disposal, that he should have constructed a Government, and in his brief administration have entered into relations with foreign States, would seem to justify what Hill Burton says of him. But to my mind the greatest proof of Wallace's eminence and power is this—that in the amnesty of 1304, when Scotland lay almost prostrate at the feet of the invader, Wallace was the sole exception to whom no mercy or quarter was to be shown—as if even Edward in the full swell of his power and supremacy felt that his Empire was not safe so long as so dangerous, so potent, and so capable an enemy was at large.

Again, whatever his talents may have been, there is something greater in great men than their talents; for the most consummate talents in themselves will not make a great man. There is in them, besides their talent, their spirit, their character, that magnetic fluid, as it were, that enables them to influence vast bodies of their fellow men, which makes them a binding and stimulating power outside the circle of their own personal fascination. That Wallace had this power we have abundant evidence. He was the first to rise and to face the oppressor. It was he who set the heather on fire. It was he who inspired the men and the events which followed. For, after all, what Wallace in his own person effected and achieved is as nothing to what he created and bequeathed—the fixed resolve of undying patriotism, the passionate, unquenchable determination of freedom, the men who were to emulate and imitate himself. Without him, in face of the formidable foe they had to face, the Scots might never have rallied for defence at all. Bruce might never have stood forth and Bannockburn might not have been fought. Scotland might have become a remote and oppressed or neglected district, without a name, or a history, or a friend; and the centuries of which we are so proud, centuries so full of energy, and passion, and dramatic history, might have passed silently and heedlessly over a dark and unknown province.

Wallace was in truth the champion who

stood forth and prevented this, who asserted Scotland as an independent country, who made or remade the Scots as a nation. It is for this that we Scotsmen must put him in the highest place. It is for this that we venerate his name now that the dark and bloody memories of his time are memories and nothing more. It is for this that we honour him when his foes are our nearest and dearest friends. And can we not condense the truth about Wallace even more compactly than this? There are junctures in the affairs of men when what is wanted is a Man—not treasures, not fleets, not legions, but a Man—the man of the moment, the man of the occasion, the man of destiny, whose spirit attracts and unites and inspires, whose capacity is congenial to the crisis, whose powers are equal to the convulsion—the child and the outcome of the storm. The type of the man is the same, though you find it under different names and different forms in different ages. It is the same whether you call it Cæsar, or Luther, or Washington, or Mirabeau, or Cavour. The crisis is a travail, and the birth of the man ends or assuages it. We recognise in Wallace one of these men—a man of fate, given to Scotland in the storms of the thirteenth century. It is that fact—the fact of his destiny and his fatefulness—that succeeding generations have instinctively recognised. It is that fact in reality that we are commemorating to-day.

There are some who have doubts and difficulties with regard to celebrations of this kind. There are some who cast doubt on the wisdom of celebrating with enthusiasm men and events of so remote a period in our history. How, they think, can you kindle enthusiasm about men or events of six centuries ago? I shall not trouble this assembly with answering such persons, except in the stanza which Burns wrote about the Solemn League and Covenant; of which there are two versions, which, with your permission, I will combine. Do you remember it?

> "The Solemn League and Covenant
> Cost Scotland blood, cost Scotland tears;
> But sacred Freedom, too, was theirs.
> If thou'rt a slave, indulge thy sneers."

APPRECIATIONS

But there is another class who urge, with more reason perhaps, that it is not timely or politic or even friendly to celebrate a victory in which the defeated foes were Englishmen. In my opinion it is no disparagement to our loyalty or our affection for England that we are celebrating the memory of the battle of Stirling and of Sir William Wallace. In the course of the long and bloody wars between the two countries England has many victories to record; but in the splendid record of her triumphs all over the world it is not worth while for her to celebrate the memory of such battles as Flodden or Dunbar. To us, however, the memory of this victory and of the man by whom it was gained does not represent the defeat of an English army, but the dawn of our national existence and the assertion of our national independence. Let us all, then, Englishmen and Scotsmen together, rejoice in this anniversary and in the memory of this hero, for he at Stirling made Scotland great; and if Scotland were not great the Empire of all the Britons would not stand where it does.

ROBERT LOUIS STEVENSON

This Appreciation of Robert Louis Stevenson was delivered at Edinburgh on December 10th, 1896. Lord Rosebery presided over what he himself called "a remarkable gathering," one which "crammed the Music Hall at four o'clock on an uncongenial winter afternoon."

ROBERT LOUIS STEVENSON

In taking this prominent position this afternoon, I feel to be something of an impostor. I never knew or saw Robert Louis Stevenson face to face, and I am speaking among numbers here who knew him from childhood almost till he left this country for good. His mother is here. How, then, can I, in her presence, and in the presence of those friends who knew him so well, pretend to take a prominent part on this occasion? My part was a perfectly simple one. I wrote to the papers a genuine inquiry. I could not but believe that in this age of memorials and testimonials some stone or cairn had been put up to the memory of Robert Louis Stevenson. I should have been confident that such a memorial had been put up but for one trifling,

APPRECIATIONS

though capital, circumstance—I had never been asked for a subscription; and therefore I came to the conclusion that there were grave doubts as to whether any such movement had taken place. My inquiry has, I suppose, landed me in this chair. But I have been trying to make out some sort of relation to the genius we commemorate to-day which should entitle me to be in this place. Somewhere or other Robert Louis Stevenson has said that the two places which appealed most powerfully to his imagination are Burford Bridge and the Hawes Inn, at Queensferry. Now, it so chances that close to both those places I have pitched my tent, or had my tent pitched for me. Burford Bridge you probably do not all know. It is a place where Keats composed part of his "Endymion"; where Nelson bade farewell to Lady Hamilton. It is near the spot where Talleyrand took refuge from the Revolution; where Miss Burney first saw her husband, and where she spent the best years of her life. The Hawes Inn, at Queensferry, you probably know much better. I do not mean in the character of *bonâ fide* travellers, but rather as

ROBERT LOUIS STEVENSON

pilgrims to a sacred haunt; for it is there that the genius of Sir Walter Scott and the genius of his successor first grasped each other by the hand; for it is in the Hawes Inn, simple structure as it is, that the first act of the "Antiquary" and the first act of "Kidnapped" are both laid. It is a solace to me to think that Sir Walter Scott certainly, and Robert Louis Stevenson I think certainly too, never saw that inn as it is now, overstridden and overridden by that monster of utility the Forth Bridge, which has added so immensely to the convenience and detracted so materially from the romance of that locality. Well, I have another claim to be here, but it is a claim that I have only in common with you all, and that is of being an ardent admirer of Robert Louis Stevenson and his work.

To-day is not the moment—we have not the time, and it would require a literary capacity to which I make no pretence—to-day is not the opportunity to enter into any review of the works of Stevenson. But there are two or three points to which, as an outside reader, I must call your attention before I sit down.

APPRECIATIONS

The first is the style of the man himself—it was a tool carefully finished and prepared by himself in order the better to work out the business to which his genius led him. I daresay many of you may think that style is a light, accidental art of inspiration which comes easily to a gifted writer. But what does Stevenson say himself? "Whenever a book or a passage particularly pleased me, in which a thing was said or an effect rendered with propriety, in which there was either some conspicuous force or some happy distinction in the style, I must sit down at once and set myself to ape that quality. I was unsuccessful, and I knew it, and tried again, and was again unsuccessful, and always unsuccessful. But at least in these vain bouts I got some practice in rhythm, in harmony, in construction, and the co-ordination of parts. I have thus played the sedulous ape to Hazlitt, to Lamb, to Wordsworth, to Sir Thomas Browne, to Defoe, to Hawthorne, to Montaigne, to Baudelaire, and Oberman." And to these he adds afterwards, in a later passage, Ruskin, Browning, Morris, Keats, Swinburne, Chaucer, Webster,

Congreve, and Thackeray; and he sums it all up by saying "*that*, like it or not, is the way to write." If a dullard were to pursue that practice which Stevenson enjoins, he would at the end of it be probably only as at the beginning a "sedulous ape." But with Stevenson there was the genius to mould what he had acquired by this painful practice. Mr. Fox said of Mr. Pitt that he himself (Mr. Fox) had always a command of words, but that Mr. Pitt had always a command of the right words, and that is a quality which strikes us so in the style of Stevenson. I do not know whether his method was easy or laborious. I strongly suspect it may have been laborious, but, whichever it was, he never was satisfied with any word which did not fully embody the idea that he had in his mind, and therefore you have in his style something suggestive, something musical, something pregnant, a splendid vehicle for whatever he had to say.

He was not satisfied with style; he infused into his style a spirit which, for want of a better word, I can only call a spirit of irony of the most exquisite kind. He, as you know, adopted a style of diction which reminds us sometimes more of Addison's *Spectator* or Steele's *Tatler* than of the easier and more emotional language of these later days. But as he put into these dignified sentences this spirit which, for want of a better word, I must call irony, he relieved what otherwise might have been heavy. Now, I think you will all recognise what I mean when I speak of this spirit of irony. You will find it in, I think, every page of his works. I do not mean that of the savage and gruesome parable which has added a household word to the English language, and which is called "Dr. Jekyll and Mr. Hyde" or "Mr. Hyde and Dr. Jekyll"; but I will take one instance from one of the works of his highest imagination, "The New Arabian Nights." He takes Rudolf out of "The Mysteries of Paris" and puts him down in London as a plump and respectable Prince of Bohemia, bent on adventure, but comfortably situated, hovering always between the sublime and the ridiculous, till the author at last makes up his mind for the ridiculous and settles him down in a cigar divan. But no one can read the account of Florizel, Prince of Bohemia, without recognising the essential quality of irony which makes Stevenson's style so potent. In some of his books he develops an even more bitter power of the same kind. In "The Dynamiter" you will find that in a form sometimes in which neither Swift nor Thackeray could be excelled. The picture of the scheming dynamiter, full of the high impulse of his mission, and constantly baffled by the cruel fate of circumstances in his efforts for an exhaustive explosion, is perhaps one of the most powerful instances of sardonic treatment to be met with in the whole history of English literature.

I cannot take instances of satire, because I should have to refer you to every page, but I will take the third point on which I wish to dwell for one moment this afternoon—it is that the dramatic, realistic power of imagination, which, as I conceive, added to the style and the spirit of lambent irony which pervades Stevenson's works, is what has raised him a head and shoulders above his fellows. Now I suppose at this moment we can all conjure to our minds some scene in one of his books which strikes us as more powerful and more imaginative than the rest. There is a scene in " The Master of Ballantrae " which, powerful as it is, has never, I confess, been a favourite of mine, because the story is so utterly repulsive from the beginning to the end—the conflict of a scoundrel against a maniac narrated by a coward. But in " The Master of Ballantrae " there is a scene which we see before us as vividly as I see your faces now, where the old steward comes out with a silver candle in each hand glaring into the still and silent night, ushering the brothers to their death struggle like a landlord handing out illustrious guests to their apartments. He walks through the night, and he holds the lights while they fight, and you next see the dead body, or seemingly dead body, of the elder lying with the wax candles flickering on each side in the silent night, and then again the steward returns, the body is gone, one wax candle has fallen down, the other is upright, still flickering over the bloodshed. Can you not all see it as you read it in the page of Stevenson? To me there seems nothing more vivid in all history. Take another scene. You remember the defence of the little pavilion on the links, the old cowardly caitiff shrinking from the result of his crimes, the clinging daughter, the brave brute who defends and despises the criminal, the unwelcome guest who chronicles it, and in the midst of that strange story of defence you remember the little Italian hat that comes skimming across the scene—surely as vivid a touch as the footprint of "Robinson Crusoe." Let me give you one more instance, and only one more. It is in that masterpiece to applaud which old age and youth combine—I mean, of course, "Treasure Island." In "Treasure Island" there are two walking-sticks—sticks that I think those who have read "Treasure Island" will never forget. There is the stick of the old blind man Pew that comes rapping, rapping through the darkness like the rattle of the snake, a sure indication of the coming curse, and there is the crutch of Long John, at once a weapon and a defence, which I think

APPRECIATIONS

will live in our memory as long as any incident.

It is a folly, it is a presumption, to try and animadvert even on the works of this great genius in so cursory a manner, but the greatness of his genius is urged against any proposal to commemorate it at this moment. We are told by those who are always critics and always objectors—and nothing in this world was ever done by critics and objectors—we are told by them that, after all, the works of Robert Louis Stevenson are his best memorials. In one sense that is undoubtedly true. No man of ancient or modern times since the beginning of the world has ever left behind him so splendid a collection of his works as has Robert Louis Stevenson—I mean not merely of what they contain, but the outward and visible form of them. But this objection, if it is worth anything, means this —that testimonials are to be confined to those who have done nothing to make themselves remembered. I know very well that the age is marching at such a pace in this direction that it will be a source of pride soon to men, women, or children to say that they have never received a testimonial. The minister as he enters and as he quits his manse is hallowed by such presents; the faithful railway porter who has been for five years at his post is honoured in the same way. No man who has lived a blameless life for ten or for twenty years can well avoid the shadow of this persecution. But, for all that, it is not for the sake of Robert Louis Stevenson that I would put up this memorial; it is for our own sakes. I do not, at any rate, wish to belong to a generation of which it shall be said that they had this consummate being living and dying among them who did not recognise his splendour and his merit. I, at any rate, do not wish that some Burns shall hereafter come, as in the case of Ferguson, and with his own scanty means put up the memorial that Ferguson's own generation was unwilling to raise.

Oh, but it is said, Why not then wait ten, or twenty, or thirty years until time shall have hallowed and mellowed his reputation? Ten, or twenty, or thirty years! Who of us can

APPRECIATIONS

afford to wait so long as that? How many of us in this hall will be alive in ten, or twenty, or thirty years? We cannot reckon on the morrow, and yet, forsooth, as a protection against our own parsimony, we are to relegate to a future generation, which shall then be the judge of the reputation of this great master—we are to leave it to a future generation to do what we are reluctant to do ourselves. At any rate, I am not willing to take any such course. I am not willing that another day, or another week, or another month should pass over our heads without our having taken some steps in the direction in which I am urging. What form any such memorial should take I cannot for my part decide. Those who knew Stevenson himself would, I think, be entitled to have the first voice in the matter. There is one thing which no one has suggested, and that is an addition to our Edinburgh statues. It is a great thing that we should be able to walk about Edinburgh and see illustrious names on pedestals and something to commemorate them on these pedestals; but I think you will agree with me, without any disrespect for some of the sculptors who have executed those statues, that if those restless spirits that possessed the Gadarene swine were to enter into the statues of Edinburgh, and if the whole stony and brazen troop were to hurry and hustle and huddle headlong down the steepest place near Edinburgh into the deepest part of the Firth of Forth, art would have sustained no serious loss. We might regret not a few of the effigies that we should have lost, but, on the whole, the city would not be the loser. I see, I think, a pained protest from the Lord Provost on my right. He is the custodian of our arts. It is not likely that the spirits of which I have spoken will carry out my proposal, and therefore my opinion seems a harmless one. But in regard to the memorial one point has struck me. There are two places in the world where Stevenson might fitly be commemorated: one is Edinburgh and one is Samoa. I suppose that in Samoa some sort of memorial is sure to be raised. But, gathering as I do Stevenson's tastes only from a perusal of his works, there seem to me to have been two passions in his life—one for Scotland, and in Scotland for Edinburgh, and one for the sea. It seems to me that, if some memorial could be raised which should appeal to his passion both for Edinburgh and for the sea, we should have done the best thing in carrying out what might have been his wishes in such a connection. But whether that be so or not, of one thing I am certain—that none of us here, if I may judge from the crowding of this hall and the attitude of this audience, are willing that the time shall pass without some adequate memorial being raised. That is, after all, the materially important point for which we are met—that we should not go down to posterity as a generation that was unaware of the treasure in our midst; and I trust that before long it will be our happiness in Edinburgh to see some memorial of Robert Louis Stevenson which shall add to the historical interest of our city, and to the many shrines of learning and of genius by which it is adorned.

GLADSTONE

The first of these Appreciations of Mr. Gladstone was delivered in the House of Lords on May 20th, 1898—the day after his death. Lord Salisbury on that occasion proposed an Address to the Queen asking that Mr. Gladstone should be accorded a public funeral, with a public monument; and the subsequent speakers in support of this motion were Lord Kimberley, the Duke of Devonshire, and Lord Rosebery—in the order named. Mr. Gladstone was buried in Westminster Abbey on May 28th, and it is there that the monument will eventually be erected.

The second Appreciation was delivered at Edinburgh on November 24th, 1898, at a meeting held in support of the National Memorial to Mr. Gladstone. As a part of that Memorial a statue is to be erected in Edinburgh. Lord Rosebery has since been appointed a member of a committee of three with whom it rests to choose the sculptor and to select the site.

GLADSTONE

I

My Lords, there would at first sight appear little left to be said after what has been so eloquently and feelingly put from both sides of the House; but, as Mr. Gladstone's last successor in office, and as one who was associated with him in many of the most critical episodes of the last twenty years of his life, your lordships will perhaps bear with me for a moment while I say what little I can say on such a subject and on such an occasion. My lords, it has been said by the Prime Minister, and I think truly, that the time has not yet come to fix with any approach to accuracy the place that Mr. Gladstone will fill in history. We are too near him to do more than note the vast space that he filled in the

APPRECIATIONS

world, the great influence that he exercised, his constant contact with all the great movements of his time. But the sense of proportion must necessarily be absent, and it must be left for a later time, and even perhaps for a later generation, accurately to appraise and appreciate that relation.

My lords, the same may also be said of his intellect and of his character. They are at any rate too vast a subject to be treated on such an occasion as this. But I may at least cite the words—which I shall never forget—which were used by the noble marquis (*Lord Salisbury*) when Mr. Gladstone resigned the office of Prime Minister, that his was "the most brilliant intellect that had been applied to the service of the State since Parliamentary government began." That seems to me an adequate and a noble appreciation; but there is also this pitiful side, incident to all mortality, but which strikes one more strongly with regard to Mr. Gladstone than with regard to any one else, and it is this—that intellect, mighty by nature, was fashioned and prepared by the labour of every day and

GLADSTONE

almost every hour until the last day of health—fashioned to be so perfect a machine, only to be stopped for ever by a single touch of the Angel of Death.

My lords, there are two features of Mr. Gladstone's intellect which I cannot help noting on this occasion, for they were so signal and so salient, and distinguished him so much, so far as I know, from all other minds that I have come into contact with, that it would be wanting to this occasion if they were not noted. The first was his enormous power of concentration. There never was a man, I feel, in this world, who at any given moment, on any given subject, could so devote every resource and power of his intellect, without the restriction of a single nerve within him, to the immediate purpose of that subject. And the second feature is one which is also rare, but which I think has never been united so much with the faculty of concentration, and it is this—the infinite variety and multiplicity of his interests. There was no man, I suspect, in the history of England—no man, at any rate, in recent cen-

APPRECIATIONS

turies—who touched the intellectual life of the country at so many points and over so great a range of years. But that was in fact and reality not merely a part of his intellect, but of his character, for the first and most obvious feature of Mr. Gladstone's character was the universality and the humanity of his sympathy. I do not now mean, as we all know, that he sympathised with great causes and with oppressed nations and with what he believed to be the cause of liberty all over the world; but I do mean his sympathy with all classes of human beings, from the highest to the lowest. That, I believe, was one of the secrets of his almost unparalleled power over his fellow men.

May I give two instances of what I mean? The first time he visited Mid Lothian we were driving away from, I think, his first meeting, and we were followed by a shouting crowd as long as their strength would permit; but there was one man who held on much longer than any of them—who ran, I should think, for two miles, and evidently had some word he was anxious to say—and when he dropped away we listened for what it might be, and it was this :—" I wished to thank you, Sir, for the speech you made to the workhouse people." I dare say not many of your lordships recollect that speech; for my purpose it does not particularly matter what its terms may have been. We should think it, however, an almost overwhelming task to speak to any workhouse audience and to administer words of consolation and sympathy to a mass who, after all, represent in the main exhaustion and failure and destitution. That is the lowest class. Let me take another instance—from the highest. I believe that the last note Mr. Gladstone wrote with his own hand was written to Lady Salisbury after a carriage accident, in which the noble marquis had been involved. It was highly characteristic of the man that, in the hour of his sore distress, when he could hardly put pen to paper, he should have written a note of sympathy to the wife of the most prominent, and not the least generous, of his political opponents. My lords, sympathy was one great feature of Mr. Gladstone's character.

APPRECIATIONS

There was another with which the noble marquis has dealt, and that I would only touch on with a single word; I mean the depth of his Christian faith. I have heard, not often, and have seen it made a subject for cavil, for sarcasm, for scoffing remarks. These remarks were the offspring of ignorance and not of knowledge. The faith of Mr. Gladstone, obviously to all who knew him, pervaded every act and every part of his life. It was the faith, the pure faith, of a child, confirmed by the experience and the conviction of manhood.

That, my lords, brings me to the only other point on which I would say a word. There was no expression so frequently on Mr. Gladstone's lips as the word "manhood." Speaking of any one—I can appeal to his friends behind me—he would say with an accent that no one who heard him could ever forget—"So-and-so had the manhood to do this"; "So-and-so had the manhood to do that"; and no one, I think, will, in the converse, ever forget the extremity of scorn which he could put into the negative phrase—"So-and-so had not the manhood to do this"; "So-and-so had not the manhood to say that." It was obvious from all he said and from all he did that that virile virtue of manhood, in which he comprehended courage, righteous daring, the disdain of odds against him—that virile virtue of manhood was perhaps the one which he put the highest. This country, this nation, loves brave men. Mr. Gladstone was the bravest of the brave. There was no cause so hopeless that he was afraid to undertake it; there was no amount of opposition that would cow him when once he had undertaken it. It was, then, faith, manhood, and sympathy that formed the triple base of Mr. Gladstone's character.

My lords, this is, as has been pointed out, an unique occasion. Mr. Gladstone always expressed a hope that there might be an interval left to him between the end of his political and of his natural life. That period was given to him, for it is more than four years since he quitted the sphere of politics. Those four years have been with him a special preparation for his death, but have they not

APPRECIATIONS

also been a preparation for his death with the nation at large? Had he died in the plenitude of his power as Prime Minister, would it have been possible for a vigorous and convinced Opposition to allow to pass to him, without a word of dissent, the honours which are now universally conceded? Hushed for the moment are the voices of criticism; hushed are the controversies in which he took part; hushed for the moment is the very sound of party conflict. I venture to think that this is a notable fact in our history. It was not so with the elder Pitt. It was not so with the younger Pitt. It was not so with the elder Pitt—in spite of his tragic end, of his unrivalled services, and of his enfeebled old age. It was not so with the younger Pitt—in spite of his long control of the country and his absolute and absorbed devotion to the State. I think that we should remember this as creditable not merely to the man, but to the nation.

My lords, there is one deeply melancholy feature of Mr. Gladstone's death, by far the most melancholy, to which I think none of my

GLADSTONE

noble friends have referred. I think that all our thoughts must be turned, now that Mr. Gladstone is gone, to that solitary and pathetic figure who, for sixty years, shared all the sorrows and all the joys of Mr. Gladstone's life; who received his every confidence and every aspiration; who shared his triumphs with him and cheered him under his defeats; who by her tender vigilance, I firmly believe, sustained and prolonged his years. I think that the occasion ought not to pass without letting Mrs. Gladstone know that she is in all our thoughts to-day. And yet, my lords—putting that one figure aside—to me, at any rate, this is not an occasion for absolute and entire and unreserved lamentation. Were it, indeed, possible so to protract the inexorable limits of human life that we might have hoped that future years, and even future generations, might see Mr. Gladstone's face and hear his matchless voice, and receive the lessons of his unrivalled experience—we might, perhaps, grieve to-day as those who have no hope. But that is not the case. He had long exceeded the span of mortal life;

APPRECIATIONS

and his latter months had been months of unspeakable pain and distress. He is now in that rest for which he sought and prayed, and which was to give him relief from an existence which had become a burden to him. Surely this should not be an occasion entirely for grief, when a life prolonged to such a limit, so full of honour, so crowned with glory, has come to its termination. The nation lives that produced him. The nation that produced him may yet produce others like him ; and, in the meantime, it is rich in his memory, rich in his life, and rich, above all, in his animating and inspiring example. Nor do I think that we should regard this heritage as limited to our own country or to our own race. It seems to me that, if we may judge from the papers of to-day, that it is shared by, that it is the possession of all civilised mankind, and that generations still to come, through many long years, will look for encouragement in labour, for fortitude in adversity, for the example of a sublime Christianity, with constant hope and constant encouragement, to the pure, the splendid, the dauntless figure of William Ewart Gladstone.

II

Mr. Gladstone's connection with Edinburgh may be divided into two portions. In the first place, as a young man it was his home, for his father resided here, and he lived here with his father; and Mr. Gladstone has more than once pointed out to me the house in Atholl Crescent where he lived with his father at that time. If it be in Atholl Crescent, and I am not mistaken, I trust it will not be one of the edifices doomed to make way for the more ambitious structure, the new City Hall. Mr. Gladstone has often talked to me about his experience in Edinburgh at that time—of the long walks he used to take with Dr. Chalmers; and on the Queensferry Road there was one particular place, which he never failed to indicate as he passed, where Dr. Chalmers's hat had blown off in one of the winds with which our climate is not unfamiliar, and where Mr. Gladstone had assisted in recovering it from the midst of a

APPRECIATIONS

ploughed field. That was the first part of Mr. Gladstone's connection with Edinburgh—if we may not claim an even earlier part in the fact of the origin of his family from Leith, which, though not integrally a portion of Edinburgh, is yet connected with Edinburgh by ties of continuity and many delightful associations.

But the second part of Mr. Gladstone's connection with Edinburgh must be within the recollection of all present. I think that none of us who were living and conscious in Edinburgh in November 1879, can forget Mr. Gladstone's return to this city. So great a transport of enthusiasm was never, I believe, seen in the case of a British subject during this century. Never was there so wild a condition of excitement so alien to the ordinary conditions of Lowland character in Scotland; never was the city, if I may so express myself, so turned topsy-turvy as it was by Mr. Gladstone's return to Edinburgh at that time. I admit that was in the main a political occasion, but I do not think that the enthusiasm was entirely, or perhaps even mainly, caused by the political character of his mission. At that time I think it was rather a tribute given by Scotsmen to one who had constantly boasted of his pure Scottish origin, of one who, at an age when most men are thinking rather of the close of life than recommencing a new era of their lives, had come down on a mission of excitement, of conversion—a mission in which the highest qualities of mind and body responded with extraordinary exuberance and strength. No doubt there was not that condition of enthusiasm on every arrival of Mr. Gladstone's subsequent to that occasion, but there were many reasons for that. For one thing, you do not welcome one daily whom you are accustomed to feel a part of yourself and almost one of yourselves; and, of course, there had been political divisions on which it is unnecessary to dwell in a non-political assembly, because as regards him they are dead, gone, and forgotten. This is no political occasion, and we should not need the presence of the last and most gallant of his political antagonists, General Wauchope, to assure us of that.

APPRECIATIONS

But after all the strife of politics is over, what remains with us of Mr. Gladstone is something beyond all politics, and which, I think, will survive all the controversies in which he was engaged. We have the memory of a matchless individuality, an oratory which has never been surpassed in our time, never perhaps been equalled in all its forms and varieties, and which, perhaps, will stand unrivalled in the history of eloquence since the great Athenian models existed. We have besides a model, which appeals to all classes and to all shades of opinion, of a life, the purity of which was never questioned, the integrity of which, in all the storms and trials of politics, was never even doubted, which I will not say popularised religion—that would be too audacious an expression—but which certainly advanced the cause of Christianity in this country as much as the sermons of thousands of men. It is unnecessary for me to add anything to what I have said. Opposite your hall there stands a testimony to his love and regard for Edinburgh in the restoration of the Mercat Cross. I am well aware that in these days testimonials and memorials are a little apt to be vulgarised. We are appealed to by daily posts for testimonials to people of whom we have never heard, and for memorials to people of whom, if we have heard, we have forgotten. But that is no reason for not contributing when there is a solid instance, as on the present occasion. By remembering Mr. Gladstone in a manner worthy of his memory, we should be raising and dignifying all memorials; we should not be associating his memory with those lower and more trivial memorials to which I have alluded. But, in any case, I think, if we do not owe it to Mr. Gladstone, we owe it to ourselves that we in Edinburgh should be foremost in contributing to keep his memory alive among mankind. We in Scotland are inclined to be clannish. We are reproached with our clannishness. We are proud of our men. Our geese are apt to be swans; but, when we have a swan, let us show that we understand it; and I think it would be derogatory to our national character, to our warm appreciation of this great man, who

APPRECIATIONS

had been bone of our bone and flesh of our flesh, if on this occasion Edinburgh does not show itself worthy of its associations with Mr. Gladstone.

LONDON

On December 7th, 1896, Sir Walter Besant delivered a lecture at the Queen's Hall, London. Most appropriately, Lord Rosebery was in the chair, since the subject—London—was one in which he has always taken a great interest. Has he not been Chairman of the London County Council? Sir Walter Besant delivered his lecture first, and Lord Rosebery's Appreciation was delivered afterwards by way of comment on what the lecturer had said.

LONDON

I should have been glad had it been possible for me to-night to confine myself to the duties — the inane and luxurious duties — of chairman of such a meeting as this, but I have been asked to express in your name our thanks to Sir Walter Besant for his lecture to-night—that is to move a vote of thanks, because it will be seconded with more authority. I came with the greatest pleasure to his lecture. It was my privilege to submit Sir Walter Besant's name to the Queen for the honour of knighthood, and I did so for this reason. There are, of course, many literary men in London, as he has reminded us—and I will break a lance with him on that point in a moment—there are many men of letters in London who have distin-

APPRECIATIONS

guished themselves by the brilliancy of their works, but I doubt if there is any man of letters in London or elsewhere whose works have produced so practical and beneficent a result as those of Sir Walter Besant. But for him the People's Palace would not, I believe, have been built, and since that time he has enriched our literature in various ways, but in no respect, in my judgment, more usefully than in those two fascinating books in which he has dealt with London and with Westminster.

London, in spite of all he may say to-night, has wanted a little interest to be attracted to it. I confess I have never felt that, in proportion to the interest which provincial towns and places feel in themselves, London has ever received an adequate notice either from the antiquary or the historian. Think what pregnant interests invest the streets of London! You cannot touch the railings of St. James's Square—hideous as those railings are, and dull as are the houses that surround them—without thinking that Johnson and Savage, hungry boys, starved by their kind mother London—

who attracted men of letters to her—walked round that square one summer night and swore they would stand by their country. I take that only as an instance. Our houses are built, in the absence of those principles you wish to revive, only to last a generation or two, but while they last should not the facts to which they have borne witness be recorded on them? I take one or two concrete instances. There was a famous building in London called the Cockpit—the Cockpit of Old Westminster Palace. The Cockpit was a famous political building at the beginning of this century. At the beginning of this century the Minister of the day used to read the Sovereign's Speech to his supporters in the Cockpit—it was not an inappropriate place considering the political controversy to which it would give rise—but it was a political place of notoriety and importance. I do not believe—I shall, of course, be contradicted tomorrow; but a public man, however humble, blossoms and buds under contradiction—I do not believe any one lives in London who can tell you where the Cockpit was, which was

APPRECIATIONS

existing at the beginning of the century, and which was as well known to Londoners as Westminster Hall. Sir Walter Besant says that he knows, but he will only give a version, and there are many versions and no proof. I will take another case. During the present century many Governments have been formed in London — all Governments are formed in London. I wonder that Sir Walter Besant did not claim that to the credit of the metropolis. In my time three if not four Governments have been formed in Carlton Terrace or Carlton Gardens—it is the same thing. I do not believe that in twenty years anybody will be able to point out the house in which those Governments were formed. In our lifetime—in the lifetime of all of us, I think I may say with confidence—three Governments have been formed in Arlington Street. How long shall we know where those Governments were formed? At any rate, no stranger, however distinguished, wandering about the streets of London, would have the faintest idea where these important transactions were carried on. I know there is a society that affixes a rare and scattered medallion on the houses that it is able to identify. I sympathise with that society, but I feel that its efforts are inadequate. I know the difficulty of identifying houses, because numbers have come so comparatively lately into use; but the London County Council, never weary in the cause of good, might yet develop a new spring of activity, and establish a historic department, which might identify to Londoners some of the sites and houses in which they could feel an interest.

But if, as I know, the overburdened ratepayer should object to this development, I do suggest that more attention should be given to making our streets of London living storehouses of history instead of being blanks of stucco, as they are at present. You, Sir Walter, said that London had never been more beautiful than it is at present. I hope that that is not true. It is, at any rate, a very guarded sentence, but it conveys so bitter and painful a reflection on the past of the metropolis that I am unwilling to accept it as true. You, in your book about London, have described

APPRECIATIONS

eloquently the brilliancy of London under the Plantagenets and the Tudors—the great palaces of the Strand, the palaces that extended far beyond even the present limit of the City—at any rate, palaces which connected London and Westminster. I cannot believe that London was not proportionately more beautiful then than it is now. I feel quite certain that the beauty of London is as yet— I hope so—only the positive quantity, and that it may be comparative and even superlative before we have done with it as a task. I have another minor quarrel with the lecturer. It is a quarrel not in the interests of history, because I have no doubt that he has history on his side; it is in the interests of morality. Why should he destroy the legend of Whittington? I have always understood that, as a French soldier is supposed to have a marshal's *bâton* in his knapsack, the London apprentice saw an encouragement of the same kind in the legend of the penniless Whittington and his cat. I beg, whatever the lecturer may feel on that point, whatever may be the crushing testimony he is able to bring forward

LONDON

against the legend of Whittington, that, in the interests of common morality and of the future of the apprentices and young men of this metropolis, he will allow to be cherished undisturbed the legend of Whittington.

I am not quite sure I am even disposed to allow that the claims of London as the mother of literature are quite well founded. Stepmother would be a better word. It is quite true that London, by the sheer and brutal force of money, and also by the libraries and scientific appliances she is able to give in such profusion, does attract within her walls a greater share of literature than that to which she is entitled. She sucks within herself the literature of other cities, and I suppose she will continue to do so as our railway system, and even our motor car system, develops. But she takes them. They have to come to her, and she has not, as a rule, treated them very well; but, considering the advantages she has, I cannot think that the roll of men of letters to which she is distinctively entitled is such a very long one as it may seem. What is the greatest name in our literature? Shake-

APPRECIATIONS

speare. He came to act in London because he got more stalls filled there than anywhere else, but we have a strong suspicion that he wrote in Warwick. Sir Walter has himself excepted in the last century the illustrious names of Scott and Burns. He need not have stopped at Scott and Burns. He might have given us Southey, one of the most fertile men of letters of that day, who never came near London except for the purposes of business. He might have given us Wordsworth, who is the poetic prophet of many, though, judging from the applause, I should say he is not so much admired as that Jack Cade who was so loudly cheered. I do not know if you will claim Browning; I am very doubtful about Browning. You certainly cannot claim Tennyson. You will not claim Byron, who was hunted out of London when he came here. You will not claim Shelley, who was obliged to live in Italy. I am not here to break literary lances with the lecturer, whom I so much admire, and I think he is bound to put forward a good case for the City he so much loves and honours; but I think he has taken a historic stretch in claiming for London any more men of letters than those who have been attracted to it other than those who have been compelled to come to it from dire necessity. I said London was a stepmother. How did you treat these men of letters in the last century? What was the line? I shall be excused if I do not give it it literally, "The Muse found Scroggen stretch'd beneath a rug." Your Parnassus was Grub Street, where the poets starved and their bowels were extracted from them by predatory booksellers.

We must not put the claims of London too high. She is the greatest city in the world. She will always be the greatest city in the world if her sons and daughters are only true to themselves. I sometimes wonder why it is that Governments in the past—we are not talking politics to-night, so I will not say Governments of the present—but it has been a source of wonder to me that Governments of the past, living in the midst of London, breathing the air of London, should have been content to leave London what it is.

APPRECIATIONS

After all, you have your problems in South Africa, you have your problems constantly arising in India, you have problems all over the world; but the greatest problem of all is that which is underneath your nose, and which, as a rule, you always ignore. I do not believe—it is a commonplace to say it—that in the history of the world there has ever been such a problem for statesmen as this of London. I am not allowed to call it a city, because the City of London is only a small part of it. But there has never been such a problem to exercise the faith and the ingenuity and the enterprise and the enthusiasm of mankind as this great conglomeration of human beings which is called London. Because it surrounds the Houses of Parliament it seems to be hardly anything to those Houses of Parliament; because it is the most present and the most pressing of problems it seems to be the one problem which Governments always determine to ignore. Developments of industry do not in any degree promise any hope of relieving the superfluous population of London or to take it elsewhere. All these developments of machinery—this new cheap motor principle for example—promise exactly the reverse. They promise diminution of employment in the country, and fresh additional flocking of the rural population into the towns. This new problem of London is not waxing less but is waxing greater. You, Sir Walter, see in London a beautiful woman. Let the beauty pass. But she is a woman, with her arms in one place, her legs in another, her head in another, and her heart in another. What is this great body of disjointed but populous parishes; what is this great desert, inhabited by neglected humanity? Is it a town, populous indeed, but remote from the seat of Empire? No; it is the seat of Empire itself. You have alluded, sir, to the enterprise which has sent forth from London great schemes of colonisation. You have drawn an eloquent and pathetic picture of the dying young King, drawn from his deathbed to see the last adventurer pass on his northern journey. But after all that is only a type of what is going on every day. The last great speech made by Lord Beaconsfield was the

APPRECIATIONS

speech with regard to the retention of Kandahar. Lord Beaconsfield rose at the end of the debate, and as was not unusual with him, threw over all the previous speakers from his own side. They had said that Kandahar was the key of India. He said : " I hear a great deal of nonsense talked about this." That was the gist of his remarks. I presume he put it more politely ; I am only speaking from memory. "I am told that the key of India is Kandahar, or that the key of India is Herat. No, my lords ; the key of India is neither one nor the other. The key of India is London." That is a true saying. But you may extend it much further than that. The key of the British Empire is London ; it is that great city in which we live. If, then, representing as it does, a population equal to that of many kingdoms converted into a small span, if then the key of the Empire as it is, it cannot merit in a greater degree the attention of statesmen of the future than it has the statesmen of the past, I can only bid you pluck up your energies and stimulate them by the remarkable lecture that we have heard this evening ; be

LONDON

proud that you are citizens of no mean city, and determine, in so far as it lies with you, it shall be not meaner, not even so mean as it is, but worthy of its central position, of its great history, and of its unmeasurable destinies.

ADDRESSES

BOOKISHNESS AND STATES-
MANSHIP

There were many societies and institutions (not all of them non-political) that invited Lord Rosebery to succeed Mr. Gladstone as their president. Amongst them was the Philosophical Institution of Edinburgh. Lord Rosebery accepted the invitation, and, on November 25th, 1898, delivered his Inaugural Address on Bookishness and Statesmanship.

BOOKISHNESS AND STATES-MANSHIP

It is difficult for me to avoid a certain feeling of sadness in standing here to-night, for it is twenty-seven years since I last delivered an Inaugural Address to the Philosophical Institution. Twenty-seven years is a long time—much has happened since then—many have gone and all are changed. In the chair was the venerable and sagacious form of Lord Colonsay, who looked as wise as Thurlow, and was probably much wiser. What a formidable listener I felt him, with his prodigious white hair and bushy white eyebrows. Few prisoners in the dock can have gazed on him with more apprehension than I on that night. Then there was Blackie; we shall miss to-night the genial calls for a speech from him, and the

ADDRESSES

not less genial response; there were Sir George Harvey, the kindly President of our Academy; Mr. Gordon, twice Lord Advocate and then Lord of Appeal; the gentle and venerable Sir William Gibson-Craig; Dr. Matthews Duncan, whose rugged manner veiled so warm a heart; George Harrison, the memory of whose excellence survives, among the best of our Lord Provosts; last and not least, the uncle and second father I so lately lost—so well known and loved in Edinburgh—the warm friend of this Institution—Bouverie Primrose. All these familiar faces which encouraged me in 1871 will not be on this platform to-night. We shall miss, too, the face of another friend, also a hearty supporter of this institution—I mean John Ritchie Findlay. Edinburgh can scarcely have had a citizen of more truly public spirit; we shall long miss him—never more than here.

It is, then, with a necessary sadness that I speak to-night after so long an interval. That is not the only reason which makes it difficult for me to thank you, as I could wish, for the honour you have done me in electing me as

BOOKISHNESS & STATESMANSHIP

your President. For I stand in the fifty-second year of your Institution as seventh on an illustrious roll. It begins with Adam Black, a great citizen and servant of Edinburgh; then comes the brilliant and wayward Christopher North. Third there comes Macaulay in the glory of the second instalment of his history. He was succeeded by Brougham, then in the commencement of decline, who was followed by Carlyle, whose connection with Edinburgh was so signal and pathetic. Then, in 1881, you chose my immediate predecessor, Mr. Gladstone, who had just in a scene of matchless enthusiasm renewed, as it were, his foothold in Edinburgh.

It makes me blush to record these names and to stand in the place of these men. But as Time and Death make havoc in the ranks of mankind, we cannot pretend to fill the gaps: we can only close them and move on. My impression, however, is that, of your Presidents, the most illustrious have only been names to you. At least during the thirty years that represent my life as your neighbour, I can recall no President of your Institution

ADDRESSES

who has taken part in its proceedings. I speak under correction, and I do not forget that Macaulay made his famous speech in 1846 on the literature of Great Britain, at a meeting of this Institution. But he was not then President, while the occasion appears to have been a convivial one, and not as now a mere feast of reason.

You have taken a new and dangerous course in electing the man on the spot, for in such a case you may have taken King Stork instead of King Log. I promise you I offer no such danger. But suppose it had been Brougham, one of my predecessors, who had lived at Dalmeny during his Presidency. He was capable each year, not merely of delivering the inaugural address, but the entire course of lectures, and I verily believe that had he been challenged, he would have insisted on doing so.

Mr. Gladstone, too, could have done the same thing. He could have proffered at once, as the great attraction, a course of lectures on Homer; and with scarcely less of zest a course of lectures on Dante. But after these were

BOOKISHNESS & STATESMANSHIP

exhausted, if indeed his lore and enthusiasm with respect to those subjects could ever have been exhausted, he could have given the entire course, on subject after subject, for winter after winter, with ever-fresh knowledge and fire, and the audiences would have packed the hall night after night, almost indifferent to the topic so long as they could watch the inexhaustible play of his features and listen to the matchless melody of his voice.

You will gather from these words that I regard Mr. Gladstone as the ideal President of this Institution; that is, had he been able to devote himself as a country neighbour to your business. That may seem small praise for one who held so commanding a place in the British Empire and the world at large. But I am only speaking of one Mr. Gladstone—there were a hundred Mr. Gladstones.

Mr. Gladstone would have been an ideal President for you, if only in the character of the constant lover and explorer of books. For I take it to be a fact beyond contradiction that Mr. Gladstone was one of the most bookish statesmen that ever lived. Or rather, to put

ADDRESSES

it differently and more accurately, no one ever attained such eminence as a statesman who was essentially so bookish a man. Sir George Cornewall Lewis was not less bookish perhaps, but he never stood on or approached Mr. Gladstone's pinnacle. He was, too, more of a book-lover and book-writer than of a statesman: sound and sagacious as was his political judgment, admirable as are his published works, he will stand higher in the field of letters than in that of practical politics.

Then there is Macaulay, one of your Presidents. On his herculean feats as a man of books I dare not dwell; I would rather give you the pleasure of reading them in his fascinating biography by his brilliant nephew. Macaulay seems to have reached his climax in India. On his voyage out he had read, he says, "insatiably, the 'Iliad' and 'Odyssey,' Virgil, Horace, Cæsar's 'Commentaries,' Bacon 'De Augmentis,' Dante, Petrarch, Ariosto, Tasso, 'Don Quixote,' Gibbon's 'Rome,' Mill's 'India,' all the seventy volumes of Voltaire, Sismondi's 'History of France,' and the seven thick folios of the

BOOKISHNESS & STATESMANSHIP

'Biographia Britannica.'" And again, in another account, he says: " I devoured Greek, Latin, Spanish, Italian, French, and English; folios, quartos, octavos, and duodecimos." And after his arrival he sums it all up by saying: " Books are becoming everything to me. If I had at this moment my choice of life, I would bury myself in one of those immense libraries that we saw together at the universities, and never pass a waking hour without a book before me." There speaks the true man of books. But unluckily Macaulay does not help us with a parallel, for in him the political side, gorgeous as were his speeches, is obscured by the literary, and it is safe to say that few of the readers of to-day, as they pore spellbound over the " Essays " and the " History," know or recollect that their author was a Cabinet Minister.

Bookishness and statesmanship are, one would think, scarcely compatible. Nothing, indeed, could seem more discordant and incompatible than the life of the library and the life of politics. The man of books may steal through life like a shadow, happy with his simple pleasures, like a caterpillar on a broad, green leaf, untortured by the travail of authorship or the candour of the critic, and leave it with his name unknown, until his library be sold, should he perchance have books to sell.

The man of politics leads possibly a more useful, certainly a more arduous career. He lives in the public eye, almost in the public grasp. Out of doors there is the reporter; in the seclusion of his home there is the interviewer, both presumably hungry to receive the ideas as they pass through his capacious brain; though some go so far as to declare that the interviewer and the reporter are less the seekers than the sought, less the pursuers than the pursued. Alert, bustling, visible, deriving even a certain popularity from the fact of being known by sight; speaking to his engagements, whether he has anything to say or whether he has not; appearing on his platform, whether he be brisk and well, or sick and sorry, like an actor, only that he has to find his own words; bringing together and keeping together, as well as may be, all sorts and conditions of men; with one eye apparently on the political weather, and the other, it is to be hoped, on his political conscience, which, by-the-bye, is usually kept for him by a number of other people—a hurricane of a life, the essential quality of which is publicity. I speak, it is to be observed, only of obvious externals, and only enough of these to indicate the natural antipathy between the life of politics and the life of books.

And yet Mr. Gladstone, who rode the whirlwind and directed the storm of politics, was bookish to an extreme degree. He had not indeed reached the superlative and morbid form of bookishness, when a man is called a bookworm. The fresh breezes of a thousand active interests prevented such a development. But with encouragement and fostering circumstance, had he been nurtured in literary traditions like his great rival, had his health been feeble, it is not difficult to imagine him a bookworm, immersed in folios, a *heluo librorum*.

But, as things were, he loved books as much

as a man may without a suspicion of bibliomania. As a matter of fact he had none of what is technically called bibliomania about him; to first editions or broad margins or vellum copies he was indifferent. Had he been a very wealthy man, even this form of the noble disease might have taken him. As it was, he loved collecting, buying, handling books. It was a joy to him to arrange with his own hands the books in the library he had founded in memory of St. Deiniol. It was a sport to him to hunt down books in sale-catalogues. It was a sacred trust to him to preserve the little treasures of his youth—a classic or two that he had at Eton, the book given to him by Hannah More.

No one could have seen him reading in the Temple of Peace, as he significantly called his study, and have deemed it possible for him to be happy in any other capacity. Those who had witnessed that sight must have felt persuaded that, when he retired from public life in 1875, nothing could ever draw him from his beloved retreat. They might well have anticipated that with old books, old friends, old trees, with a hundred avenues of study to complete or explore, with a vast experience of life and affairs to discuss, with trees to cut and plant and worship—for he was a tree-worshipper as well—and above all, with the vital care and responsibility of a living faith pervading him, he might well rest and be thankful.

All this might have been safe enough to predict of an ordinary or even remarkable man. But Mr. Gladstone was a great deal more than a remarkable man; he was a number of remarkable men. And as soon as he heard the clash of a conflict, in which he saw, or thought he saw, the righteous fighting the unrighteous, the fighting Gladstone could not restrain himself, and left his tent for the battle, taking the bookish Gladstone somewhat reluctantly with him.

It was, then, his extraordinary energy, enthusiasm, and faith in great causes that were the salt that prevented his stagnation into mere bookishness. But he had another safeguard still. It was his principle in reading to make his exports balance his imports—he

ADDRESSES

took in a great deal, but he put forth a great deal. His close study of a book was pretty sure to precede an article on that book. It was impossible for him under this principle to sink into the mere passive and receptive reader. I remember, too, his applying it in conversation to an ecclesiastical statesman for whom he had a real admiration. "I daresay," he remarked in answer to some disparaging criticism as to thinness of matter, "I daresay that as he has to speak so often, he has to put forth more than he can take in to replace his output." I do not doubt, then, that his principle of balancing exports and imports would have kept his mind active, even had it not possessed other animating and quickening principles.

I reckon over all this to explain, as far as I can explain, the paradox of a bookish statesman, of a bookman (to use the old expression) who was at the same time a man of practical business and affairs: one of the rarest of all combinations.

Let us test this assertion by instances—let us take the case of Prime Ministers as an

BOOKISHNESS & STATESMANSHIP

average representation of men of affairs. If you glance roughly over the Prime Ministers since the beginning of the last century, you will find Harley as a book-lover, but even he was rather a collector than a reader, and can hardly be called an eminent statesman. Bolingbroke, who was perhaps Prime Minister for a few hours, was a book-lover after his fall, or said he was. But in his days of office and youth and frankness, though he came a brilliant scholar from Eton, he cannot have much consorted with books. Stanhope had a library which still exists intact at Chevening, preserved in a separate room—a priceless example of the book collection of a Minister in the early eighteenth century. Sunderland founded a great library, mainly, I think, of editions of the classics, which went from Althorp to Blenheim with the elder branch, afterwards replaced at Althorp by an even nobler collection. Then we come to Walpole. The sublime solace of books, which soothed even the gnawing ambition of his fiercest enemy, was denied to him. No one deplored this after his resignation more than himself. Once on finding a friend reading in his own library at Houghton he expressed this feeling. "I wish," he said, "I took as much delight in reading as you do; it would be the means of alleviating many tedious hours in my present retirement; but, to my misfortune, I derive no pleasure from such pursuits." And again in the same room he said to Henry Fox: "You can read. It is a great happiness. I totally neglected it when I was in business, which has been the whole of my life, and to such a degree that I cannot now read a page —a warning to all Ministers." And for his neglect of one branch of literature, he gave one pregnant and famous reason: "Do not read history, for that I know must be false." But he found in his country retirement one resource which he shared with Mr. Gladstone, who had all or nearly all the resources, for both statesmen delighted in trees. "My flatterers here," wrote Walpole in a passage of such pathetic beauty, that one can scarcely credit his deficiency of literary taste, "my flatterers here are all mutes. The oaks, the beeches, the chestnuts, seem to contend which shall best please the lord of the manor. They cannot deceive, they will not lie." And the tree was as living to Gladstone as to Walpole, but with him it was only one of innumerable living interests.

From Walpole onwards we meet with no bookish Prime Minister till we get to Lord Grenville. He was, no doubt, a man of strong literary tastes, but does not come into competition with Mr. Gladstone as an omnivorous reader, much less with the eminence, fulness, and energy of Mr. Gladstone's public life. But a friend who used to visit him gives a picture of his old age, sitting summer and winter on the same sofa with his favourite books on the shelves just over his head; Roger Ascham among them; Milton always within reach. He, at any rate, in his sixty-sixth year was clear as to the choice between literature and politics. A Minister leaves him to go to his office. "I would rather he was there than I," says Grenville. "If I was to live my life over again," he continued with a sigh, "I should do very differently."

The next possibly bookish Prime Minister

was Canning; but, with a literary side all his life, he was only Prime Minister for a few months. Beyond Canning I hardly dare to go. Melbourne, indeed, was a great reader, and, like Mr. Gladstone, a great reader of theology; but he left behind him a library of odd volumes, which puts him out of the category of book-lovers. Sir Robert Peel, like some of the statesmen of the last century, came to the business of politics as a brilliant specimen of Oxford scholarship. Lord John Russell was perhaps more a writer than a reader of books. The only book, I think, mentioned by Lord Palmerston in his correspondence is "Coningsby." Then we come to the author of "Coningsby," "born," as he says, "in a library," more bookish perhaps than Mr. Gladstone in early, and less in later life. But all this is dangerous ground; we are passing from the land of shadows into actual life; I know not where to stop. But once when I was a child, I was taken to see Hatfield. In the library we saw a tall thin figure carrying a huge volume. The housekeeper paused with awe, saying, "That is

BOOKISHNESS & STATESMANSHIP

Lord Robert Cecil." It was a bookish figure, then outside politics, but now Prime Minister.

I turn my face briskly from the alluring present to the prudent past. Shall we find outside the list of Prime Ministers many in the secure latitudes of the past who compete with Mr. Gladstone, as being bookish men in high Ministerial office ? Clarendon is beyond my horizon. But there is, of course, Addison, who was a Secretary of State, but so indifferent a one as to fail entirely in one point of comparison. There is Bolingbroke, to whom I have already alluded, and who would require a volume to himself. There is Burke, a mighty force in politics and in letters, but never in such office as to demonstrate himself a great Minister ; any more than Charles James Fox, who held office for too short a time. But Charles Fox had a real passion for literature, could talk of it the whole day and over the whole range of it. He, I think, in a real love of books approaches most nearly to Mr. Gladstone, and both had a common devotion to Homer. Homer was the author that Charles Fox most loved to read ; but he would also read all the novels that he could get hold of. In conversation he would range over almost the whole field of literature with zest and passion, and without apparently once straying into politics. A friend has recorded how in a day he would discuss Homer and Virgil, Æschylus and Euripides, Milton and Massinger, Pope and Addison, Gibbon and Blackstone, Sophocles and Shakespeare, Metastasio, Congreve and Vanbrugh, Cowper, Fielding and Burns. He almost convinces himself that Burns is a better poet than Cowper. But he concludes by saying finely enough that poetry is the great refreshment of the human mind. No one surely can deny that Fox was a man of books. But he is not a parallel for the combination which in Mr. Gladstone was unique, in that he was only a Minister for a few months; once under circumstances dubious, if not sinister, and once when he was dying. He was not then, as my predecessor was, carrying on simultaneously on parallel lines a great career as a statesman in office and a delightful life in a library. Moreover, all this, except in the

BOOKISHNESS & STATESMANSHIP

case of the history of James II. which slumbers on our shelves in majestic quarto, was without any result. Nor was there in him, as I read him, the passionate concentration and practical application of reading that we saw in Mr. Gladstone. "His favourite Sultana Queen," as with his royal ancestor, "was sauntering," and sauntering was abhorrent and impossible to Mr. Gladstone. Charles Fox, at any rate, after ruining himself at cards, could sit down and derive an instant solace from Theocritus. And indeed, as a rule, the public men of the last century seem to have been fairly well equipped in what Captain Dugald Dalgetty called "the humanities"; they would have blushed not to understand, or not to appear to understand, a Latin quotation; they could bandy and bet over them as Pulteney did with Walpole, but they do not seem to have been men of books. There are perhaps two signal exceptions, statesmen of eminence and power in the first rank, who were also men of books, and I do not feel perfectly sure even of one of these two; I mean Carteret and Chesterfield.

ADDRESSES

The great exemplar in the eighteenth century of the combination of literature and politics was undoubtedly Chesterfield. Perhaps, indeed, the only startling deficiency in his intellectual equipment was his unaccountable ignorance of the mother tongue of that Hanoverian dynasty which he was so anxious to serve. There his rival Carteret had the advantage of him, and it was not slight. But Carteret never pretended to, or indeed would have cared for, the sovereignty in the literary world that was occupied by Chesterfield. And, moreover, their habits were very different. One loved cards, and the other wine. But it was the delight of Chesterfield to combine his gambling with polite society, until deafness excluded him altogether from conversation.

Carteret, on the other hand, kept a large, plain, hospitable table, where burgundy flowed freely. He was, however, the best Greek scholar of his age. He had left Christ Church with a rich store of classical learning. To this he added a consummate knowledge, not merely of modern politics, but of modern

BOOKISHNESS & STATESMANSHIP

languages. He is said to have been at his ease in French, Spanish, Italian, German, Swedish, and Portuguese. But he seems always to have been faithful to his first love of the classics. On his deathbed, indeed, he repeated with sonorous emphasis six lines from the twenty-second book of the "Iliad," for he, scarcely less than Mr. Gladstone, worshipped and cherished Homer. "Ah, friend," he said in the words of Sarpedon (I quote from Mr. Andrew Lang's translation), "ah, friend, if, once escaped from this battle, we were for ever to be ageless and immortal, neither would I fight myself in the foremost ranks, nor would I send thee into the war that giveth men reason ; but now—for assuredly ten thousand fates of death do every way beset us, and these no mortal may escape nor avoid—now let us go forward."

There is something sublime in the dying statesman's signing his last papers with these words on his lips ; it is in the old grand style, and we may infer perhaps that the thoughts of his old age were those of Grenville, and that he repented him of the choice that he had made. But words spoken in sickness can scarcely represent the judgment or passion of the man entering life. Carteret's was too ardent a spirit to refrain from active and even fiery ambition. It would be tempting to draw his character, one of the most interesting of his century. But that would be outside my compass; I am only asserting his character as a man of learning and a man of affairs. Of absolute bookishness he was strongly suspected, and classics were to be found, it was said, in his dressing-room. But I am content to make the claim that he was eminently and concurrently a scholar and a statesman.

It is perhaps difficult to understand on what claim or merit was based Chesterfield's literary throne. That he occupied one is sufficiently evident from the fact that Johnson, who was no courtier, had thought of dedicating his Dictionary to him. A few essays, more or less anonymous, were all the productions known to his contemporaries—essays which appeal but little to us. His letters to his son and to his godson, on which rest his fame, and which indeed, to some of us, seem

BOOKISHNESS & STATESMANSHIP

dreary enough, were posthumous. In these letters, however, we find symptoms of his bookishness. From them we may suppose him versed in the literature of his own country, of France, and perhaps of Italy. In England his idol is Bolingbroke. In France he sees such perfection, that one would infer that he worships there a literary polytheism. But his verdict on Italian literature separates him for ever from my predecessor in your Presidency. The only Italian poets that he thinks worth reading are Tasso and Ariosto. He deliberately excludes Dante, a veto which seems an abiding slur on his perception; and which, in Mr. Gladstone's judgment, would have constituted him a sort of literary outlaw. Moreover, in spite of Chesterfield's undoubted love of reading, he places on record an injunction which strikes him altogether out of the category of thorough bookishness. " Lay aside," he solemnly says, " the best book whenever you can go into the best company; and, depend upon it, you change for the better." Perhaps, when we remember that the best society, in the highest sense, is rarely attainable, he is right. But then we might not all agree as to what constitutes the best society. I am not going to discuss the point to-night, but I strongly recommend it to the debating societies of our University, which, after a protracted existence, must be gaping like stranded oysters for fresh subjects of polemic. It is in any case a hard saying, and must be held to exclude Chesterfield from the straitest sect of the worshipful company of bookmen.

Mr. Gladstone would certainly not have subscribed to it in this bare and absolute form. But, in any case, were Chesterfield ten times as bookish as he was, he would not have equalled Mr. Gladstone any more in that quality, than in the length and splendour of his public career. There is no parallel between them; I only take Chesterfield because I can think of nobody else.

I believe, then, as I have said before, that nowhere in history, so far as I know, is there an instance of so intensely bookish a man as Mr. Gladstone, who was at the same time so consummate a man of affairs. I limit myself

BOOKISHNESS & STATESMANSHIP

to the two last centuries as alone offering conditions analogous to those in which Mr. Gladstone lived. And I must again guard myself by saying that I am not now speaking of the mere collection of libraries, in which several, perhaps many, statesmen have surpassed him. I mean by bookishness the general love of books—reading, buying, handling, hunting them. The combination in his case is, I believe, unique, and will probably remain so. Day by day the calls of public life become more and more exacting, absorbing, imperious. Each fresh development of them makes them more and more unsuitable for the student and the recluse. Literature is constantly becoming less and less necessary for the politician. During the first half of this century a classical quotation was considered the indispensable ornament of a parliamentary speech. Greek quotations passed long ago into space — found their way back perhaps to ancient Hellas — and even Latin quotations may be said to have been buried with Mr. Gladstone. The Blue-book has superseded Homer, and

ADDRESSES

Virgil is swamped in the "Statesman's Year Book."

We shall understand all this better perhaps by abandoning the task of seeking analogies for Mr. Gladstone's love of books, and by taking the greatest imaginable contrast to him.

There has of late been given to the world the remarkable biography of a remarkable man—the late Charles Stewart Parnell. For ten years Mr. Parnell filled the largest space in Mr. Gladstone's public life, perhaps in English public life: his position in his own country it is unnecessary to define or describe. What was the secret of this prodigious success? It has never been revealed, perhaps it never will be, perhaps it never can be. One point, however, is clear, that it was due to a character and temperament the exact antipodes of Mr. Gladstone's. The one ardent, enthusiastic, fascinating, exuberant in his sympathies and studies, clutching with both hands at every fruit and blossom of the tree of knowledge; the other icy, silent, superstitious, concentrated, a political enigma of the pro-

BOOKISHNESS & STATESMANSHIP

foundest interest. But to-night we are concerned with only one aspect of each. Mr. Parnell professed a general ignorance, even of a subject that concerned him so nearly as Irish history. And this strange want of the knowledge to be found in books appears all through his life. "I am very ignorant," he once said to his biographer, who smiled incredulously. "Yes," he continued, "I mean what I say. I am very ignorant of these things. I have read very little, but I am smart, and can pick up information quickly." On another occasion he had engaged to lecture on Irish history at Cork. Parnell said to a friend, "I really do not know anything about Irish history. Have you got any books I can read?" The day of the lecture came; it was to be delivered at eight o'clock. At a quarter to eight, when dinner was over, Parnell said, "Now I must read up the history," and he asked for some writing-paper and the historical books. He arrived at the hall at 9.15, was received with enthusiasm, and got through his lecture successfully. That anecdote seems to me profoundly interesting for many reasons. The nerve, the coolness, the declared ignorance of Irish history, and the enthusiasm of an audience that had been waiting for an hour and a quarter, are all equally remarkable.

This carries me far beyond my contention that bookishness and statesmanship are rarely compatible, for it appears to point to a complete immunity from books as the secret of political success.

And yet is it so ? Is not Parnell a phenomenon and an exception to all rules ? Is not the true life of the politician the balance of action and study—study not merely a preparation for action, but of literature as a recreation ? Among the great men of action we recall Frederick's love of letters and Napoleon's travelling library. Among statesmen we think of Pitt's sofa with its shelf of thumbed classics ; and of Fox, a far more ardent lover of books, exchanging them and his garden for the House of Commons almost with tears ; and of Gladstone's Temple of Peace.

And surely, even if it be not the best, it is

BOOKISHNESS & STATESMANSHIP

the happiest way. There is little vestige of happiness in the life of Parnell. There is not perhaps too much happiness in the life of any statesman. But no one who knew him could think Mr. Gladstone otherwise than happy, and one of the main sources of his happiness was his bookishness. We may indeed say more than that. We may say that where, as in his case, the mind absorbs and uses the books, and the books do not cloud and embarrass the mind, the purpose of the statesman and the eloquence of the orator gather colour and force from books as a river takes the hues and gathers up the springs of the regions it traverses. But even here I must guard myself once more : Mr. Gladstone was a prodigy, and no rule deduced from his life can be absolute for others.

And so, gentlemen, I leave you to form your judgment for yourselves, by the light of your own reason, by the guidance of your instinct. For, in truth, all ends in that. All the lectures and addresses, inaugural or otherwise, of the Philosophical Institution, or any other institution, athenæum, or college, can only help you to form your own judgment, and to rely on yourselves. Read books like Gladstone, or disdain books like Parnell; as to that you must judge for yourselves. There is no royal road to success in public life; what suits one will not suit another. But of this at least I am sure, that, putting politics and success equally out of the question, if a man wants to develop his faculties to the utmost advantage, and to combine the greatest amount of work with the greatest amount of happiness, he cannot do better than imitate, so far as he is able, the methods of study, the economy of time, and the regularity of life practised by my illustrious predecessor in the Presidency of the Philosophical Institution.

THE DUTY OF PUBLIC SERVICE

On October 25th, 1898, Lord Rosebery delivered his Presidential Address to the Associated Societies of the University of Edinburgh. On the principle that one good Scot deserves another, the chair was taken by Mr. Arthur Balfour, who was there not merely to show that the occasion was a non-party one, but also because he happens to be the Chancellor of the University.

THE DUTY OF PUBLIC SERVICE

I AM not sure that this sumptuous Hall with which the generous Mr. M‘Ewan has endowed this University is in the nature of an unmixed benefit. It makes too much of an occasion like this. To tell the truth, as I look around me and see this vast audience, I am irresistibly reminded of the most dismal moment that can occur in a man's life—the moment when he is about to deliver a Rectorial Address. Happily, there are one or two considerations which reassure me. One is, that the altar is already lighted for another victim, whose sacrifice, in the natural course of things, cannot long be delayed. My other comfort, sir, is that you are in the chair, because, to put it on no higher ground, the Chancellor is never present at a

ADDRESSES

Rector's Address. The same firmament cannot hold two such planets, and therefore, when I see you there, I am perfectly certain that the impression I derive from this audience is an erroneous one, and that I am not going to deliver a Rectorial Address. Well, sir, we welcome you here for every reason. We are glad to see you in your place as Chancellor. We are glad to see you on any plea in Edinburgh; and what I am happy to think of is this, that we can ensure you in that chair for the next fifty minutes what, perhaps, you can obtain nowhere else, a period of unbroken repose, untroubled by colleagues, untroubled by Cabinets, undisturbed even by boxes or telegrams; and if you, sir, will take my advice, you will take advantage of that repose. But, gentlemen, if I can explain why the Rector is not here, and why the Chancellor is, it is perhaps more difficult to explain to myself why I am here. It is partly, no doubt, because in an unwary moment I accepted this responsible office, which has such onerous duties. But it is also due to another circumstance, that, when we were last in this Hall, you

THE DUTY OF PUBLIC SERVICE

invited me, somewhat clamorously, to address you. I am a person, however, accustomed to walk in the established order of things: I could not interrupt the programme. It would neither have been *dulce* nor *decorum* for me to speak on that occasion. But to-night I am here to respond to that invitation. To-night, it is perhaps *decorum* that I should speak; and if it can ever be *dulce* to make a speech, it is *dulce* on this occasion. But, at any rate, let us be quite clear in our understanding. I am not going to deliver a Rectorial Address— nothing so elaborate, nothing so educational. Simply, I trust, it will be a short speech on common-sense lines, and without rising to the heights of the other occasion to which I have alluded.

Now, sir, with a view to the adequate performance of my functions to-night, I have been reading the address of my predecessor, our friend Professor Masson, and as I am quite sure that you have all read Professor Masson's Address too, it will not be necessary on this occasion to condescend upon details. You know more than I do about the constitu-

ADDRESSES

tion of these Societies, and you may perhaps be able—which I am not—to decide as to their relative antiquity. But there is one sinister and significant sentence in Professor Masson's Address to which I commend your attention. He says that for sixteen years the post of President was vacant, because no one could be found willing to accept the responsibility of delivering the Presidential Address. Now, if that does not move your compassion for the person who has that courage, your hearts must be harder than adamant. There is another sentence which produced a great awe and effect upon my mind. It is said that the Societies had done much good work which did not seem affected materially by the absence or the presence of their President, and, as a specimen of that good work, he said that no less than twenty thousand essays had been delivered to the Societies in the course of their existence. Twenty thousand essays! That is a hard saying. Twenty thousand essays, blown into space! And it leads further to this appalling calculation, that if a gentleman hearing of the Associated Societies

THE DUTY OF PUBLIC SERVICE

had determined to improve his mind by reading these essays, and had determined to read one every day before breakfast, it would have been sixty years before he had accomplished the task. Now, that to me, I confess, is not the precious fact in connection with these Societies. What to me is precious is this, that they garnered up so much of what is illustrious, both in regard to memories and to men in connection with Edinburgh. Take, for example, the Dialectic Society, which was founded in 1787. Well, how brilliant was Edinburgh in 1787! A race was growing up in your Schools and in your Universities which was destined afterwards, through the means of the *Edinburgh Review*, to influence largely both the taste and the policy of these Islands. They were at that time pretty young, the most of them. Cockburn—Lord Cockburn—was being flogged every ten days at the High School, every ten days, according to a minute and pathetic calculation that he has left behind him. Jeffrey—Lord Jeffrey—was at that time entering Glasgow University in his fourteenth year; and as for Lord

ADDRESSES

Brougham, he was at that moment commencing a career of conflict by a struggle with a master of his class, in which, I need hardly say, Brougham came off victorious. Dugald Stewart was lecturing at that time, not merely to Edinburgh, but to the kingdom, and almost to the world at large, and Edinburgh was the centre to which all the intellect of Great Britain might, without exaggeration, be said to have gravitated. At that time the English Universities were slumbering. Jeffrey had indeed taken a taste of Oxford, but liked it not. His biographer carefully says that "his College was not distinguished by study and propriety alone." This shocked Jeffrey, and he left it. But in any case these were the golden days of Edinburgh. It was then unrivalled as an intellectual centre, unrivalled in a sense that it can never be again. Some will say that all that is gone. Well, as for the intellectual supremacy, that could not survive in the general awakening of the world. But what I also fear has gone, is the resident, inherent originality which then distinguished our city. Railways and the Press

THE DUTY OF PUBLIC SERVICE

have made that impossible; for, after all, true originality can scarcely exist but in the backwaters of life. The great ocean of life smooths and rolls its pebbles to too much the same shape and texture. Those famous judges of whom we read, with something between a smile and a tear—Braxfield and Eskgrove and Newton and Hermand—are just as impossible in these days as the black bottles with which they stimulated their judicial attention on the bench. They are as impossible as that cry of "Gardez-loo," which meant so much to the passer-by on the streets. Well, after all, we must take the rough with the smooth, and the good with the bad. "Gardez-loo" itself was only the symbol of hideous physical impurities, which we none of us should regret; and perhaps even some of those social glories over which we are so accustomed to gloat in the past, might not have been entirely agreeable had we to realise them in the present. Take these old judges whom I mentioned. They are very picturesque and interesting figures; but I am not sure that any of us could have faced them in the character of a defendant or an accused person without a qualm, more especially if we were opposed to them in politics, and even—if tradition lies not—even if we were their opponents at chess. And if we were in that unfortunate and perhaps discreditable position, we should go and seek our legal adviser, not, as now, in the decorous recesses of Queen Street or of George Street, but, as Colonel Mannering went to seek him, at Clerihugh's, enjoying "high jinks" in the midst of a carousal, from which he could hardly tear himself for matters of the most vital import to his client.

Well, of course it is impossible to read Lord Cockburn's "Memorials of His Time" —and I hope that you all do read it, and read it at least once a year, because no resident of Edinburgh can properly enjoy his city without reading Lord Cockburn once a year—it is impossible to read Lord Cockburn without seeing that he was an optimist. But even he says of the Edinburgh of his time— which he says was so unrivalled—even he describes it as "always thirsty and unwashed."

THE DUTY OF PUBLIC SERVICE

Well, I am not quite sure when I read that description if we should have thought the Edinburgh of 1787 as delightful as he did. I hardly venture to risk myself in this line of conjecture. Should we all have appreciated Jeffrey as much as he did? That must remain in the realms of the unknowable and the unknown. But there is worse behind. There is even treason talked about the divine Sir Walter Scott. In that very delightful book which furnishes so much leisurely reading for the Scotsman or the Scotswoman, or for anybody—I mean " Memoirs of a Highland Lady "—I came upon this sentence, which I have never since been able to digest. It says about Sir Walter Scott—" He went out very little," and when he did go, that " he was not an agreeable gentleman, sitting very silent, looking dull and listless unless an occasional flash lit up his countenance. It was odd, but Sir Walter never had the reputation in Edinburgh that he had elsewhere." Gentlemen, I veil my face; I cannot get over that, till I remember that a prophet is never a prophet in his own country, and there may

ADDRESSES

have been people, even in Edinburgh, who did not think of Sir Walter as we do. But I do not mention all these disagreeable considerations as sheer iconoclasm and blasphemy. No, gentlemen, it is in a very different spirit that I lay them before you. I lay them before you as with a sort of inward groan. They are to me a sort of philosophic potsherd with which I scrape myself. It is in the attempt to comfort myself for living in the Edinburgh of the end of the nineteenth century, and not in the Edinburgh of the eighteenth or the seventeenth or the sixteenth century, that thus I endeavour to recall these things, and console myself anew.

Well, I think then there are some circumstances which we should bear in mind before we give way to the wish to exchange new Edinburgh for old Edinburgh. At any rate, there are some circumstances that should discount our enthusiasm. But, indeed, in any case it would not be possible for us of the Associated Societies to concentrate all our interest in Edinburgh as our forefathers did. In the first place, our students, our members,

THE DUTY OF PUBLIC SERVICE

are by no means all Scotsmen. They come from England, and from all over the world. They come here, many of them, to learn arts which they mean to practise and to exercise elsewhere, so that it would be impossible for them to remain in Edinburgh; if they did, indeed, I think that some professions in Edinburgh would be somewhat glutted and overstocked. But, in the second place, there is the railroad, which equally prevents it—the railroad, which has so profoundly stirred up our people, which has so inspired them with the fever of travel, makes concentration in our old capital impossible. By thousands are the strangers that it brings in and takes out of Edinburgh every day, and indeed, as regards its effect on our town, it is something like that of the pipes which convey the water of some hushed and inland loch away to the boisterous strife of cities, and again away from the cities to the eternal ocean. The students of that Edinburgh which was once so difficult to reach and to leave are now whirled away into a thousand whirlpools of civilisation; they can no longer huddle around and try to blow

ADDRESSES

up the embers of that ancient Edinburgh which we can only revive in imagination. But of Edinburgh as it exists—the historical, the beautiful, the inspiring—I trust they have taken and are taking a deep draught and a long memory. They are here at the most critical and the most fruitful period of their lives; and sure am I that, whether they wish it or not, they will bear away from this place a seal and a mark and a stamp which can leave them only with life itself.

But, gentlemen, I go a little further in this sense, and I believe that, even if the students could remain in Edinburgh and concentrate themselves here, it would be bad for Edinburgh and bad for Scotland, but bad also for the Empire. We in Scotland wish to continue to mould the Empire as we have in the past —and we have not moulded it by stopping at home. Your venerable Principal is an instance in point. And we have even a nearer object-lesson in two returning Viceroys from Canada and from India; Aberdeen—from Canada, where he is by-and-bye to be replaced by a Minto—and Elgin—the second Elgin—from

THE DUTY OF PUBLIC SERVICE

India. Well, I say then that it is not the Edinburgh of Cockburn alone that I wish you to bear in your thoughts to-night, but rather the Edinburgh which has dispersed her sons all over the Empire, the assiduous mother and foster-mother of the builders of our Empire. From the time of Dundas, who almost populated India with Scotsmen, that has always been the function of Scotland; and I look, then, to my colleagues of the Associated Societies not merely as going forth to their several professions and callings in life, but as going forth as potential Empire-builders, or at least as Empire-maintainers.

You will, gentlemen, when you go forth from these learned precincts and enter upon the actual business of life—you will have in the course of your lives to help to maintain and to build that Empire. You may think that it may be in a small and insignificant manner, not more than the coral insect within the coral reef. But recollect that the insect is essential to the reef; and it is not for any man of himself to measure what his direct utility may be to his country. I will tell you why you must in your way exercise those functions. The British Empire is not a centralised Empire. It does not, as other Empires, hinge on a single autocrat or even on a single Parliament, but it is a vast collection of communities spread all over the world, many with their own Legislatures, but all with their own Governments, and, therefore, resting, in a degree which is known in no other State of which history has record, on the intelligence and the character of the individuals who compose it. Some Empires have rested on armies, and some on constitutions. It is the boast of the British Empire that it rests on men. For that reason it is that I speak to you to-night as men who are to have your share in the work of the Empire, small or great, humble or proud. That is—unless you go absolutely downwards—your irresistible and irrevocable function. Now, it is quite true that your share in that work may not be official, but even then I would ask, why not? There never was in the history of Great Britain, or, I suspect, of the world, so great a call as now upon the energies and

THE DUTY OF PUBLIC SERVICE

intelligence of men for the public service, and that call, as you, sir, know, is increasing daily. Within Great Britain in my own memory the change in that respect has been very remarkable. What was called the governing class—and which is to some extent the governing class still—when I was a boy had very simple public functions in comparison with those which devolve upon the present race. They went into Parliament as a rule, and they had Quarter Sessions. But Parliament in those days was a very different business from what it is now, and Quarter Sessions—were Quarter Sessions. The burden of Parliament has now indefinitely and almost hopelessly increased, as you, sir, I doubt not, would be willing to depose on oath, if necessary. That takes up for these Islands some five hundred and seventy more or less trained intelligences. Then there is the House of Lords, which takes up some—I am not sure of the figures—some five or six hundred more. I do not wish to claim that the House of Lords takes up the whole time of its members; I merely wish to point out that that, again, takes a

ADDRESSES

part of the time, at any rate, of some five or six hundred more of our governing class. Then there is a new institution—the London County Council. That is a body whose work is not less absorbing than that of the House of Commons. It lasts much longer; it is much more continuous, and, though not nearly so obtrusive, it is quite as arduous. Well, that consists of a small body of a hundred and thirty-eight members, who must all, who should all, be highly qualified for the function of governing a nation which is not smaller than many self-governing kingdoms. Then there are the municipalities — great and small. These, no doubt, have to some extent always existed, but not in their present form. A new spirit has been breathed into these somewhat dry bones. The functions of a municipality are sought by men of the highest intelligence; they are not merely sought by men of the highest intelligence, but absorb a very great proportion of the time of these men. They are changed altogether in spirit and in extent. And it is notable now to remark how many men in business plead as

THE DUTY OF PUBLIC SERVICE

a just excuse from entering either the House of Commons or municipal work that they cannot spare the time from the necessary prosecution of their business which would enable them to join in those absorbing avocations. The municipalities of to-day—I know not how many men whose time they absorb—but they are very different from the municipalities of my boyhood, and I suspect that if a Town Councillor of forty or fifty years ago were to present himself in a Town Council of to-day, he would regard their work with astonishment, and they perhaps might look at him with some surprise. Then there are County Councils, District Councils, Parish Councils—all bodies new within the last few years—not all of them absorbing the whole time of their members, but requiring, at any rate, the services of many trained intelligences to keep their work in proper order and without arrears. Then there are the Government Departments, which swallow up more and more men, and pass them on very often to higher employments. Their work is indefinitely and incalculably increasing. I will give

ADDRESSES

you one symptom. The Foreign Office this year has obtained one new Under-Secretary; and the addition of an Under-Secretary is a cry of distress indeed. Well, the Colonial Office, I see from the papers, is also about to demand an Under-Secretary, and what that means of increase in the subordinate departments is more than I can rightly calculate. But in truth, gentlemen, the whole matter is typified in the constitution of the Cabinet. The present Cabinet requires nineteen men to do what was done by half a dozen in the days of Mr. Pitt.

Why do I quote these figures? I quote them to show the enormous drain that the State makes on our intelligent population, besides the drain that it makes both for military and naval purposes. Napoleon was said to drain his population for his warlike purposes. We may be said, if not to drain, at least to skim ours very frequently for the purposes of administration. Now what I have been telling you relates to Great Britain alone. There is, besides Ireland. Well, I am not going to touch on Ireland. In the first place,

THE DUTY OF PUBLIC SERVICE

it is a different system of administration, and one with which I am not so conversant; and, in the second place, this is at present a harmonious meeting, and I have discovered that there is no topic so likely to terminate the harmony of a meeting as that of the administration or the government of Ireland. I pass beyond that. Outside Great Britain and Ireland there is an enormous drain on our population for administrative purposes. There is India, which takes so many of our young men, and trains them so incomparably well for every sort of administrative work. There is Egypt, which is, of course, on a different footing, but which is also very large in her requirements. There is Africa — not self-governing Africa, but the rest of our Africa, with its territories, its spheres of influence, and so on, all requiring men to mould them into shape, not necessarily men belonging to the Civil Service or men of formula, but muscular Christians, who are ready to turn their hands to anything. Then, besides that and beyond that, there are the outer Britains, if I may so call them, the great commonwealths

ADDRESSES

outside these Islands which own the British Crown—whether Crown Colonies, in which case they require administrators, or self-governing Colonies, in which case they require the whole appurtenance of Parliament, Courts of Law, Ministers, and so forth. Then, outside that again, there are our Diplomatic and Consular Services. Well, I do not suppose there ever was in the history of the world half the demand that there is at this hour within the British Empire for young men of ability and skill and training to help to mould that Empire into shape. Never were there so many paths of distinction open within that Empire; while to those who would share in that task of Empire-building, and who would do it, not with the hope of amassing much riches, but in a high missionary spirit, never was there such an opportunity as opens at the present moment.

Of course, the base of all this tremendous work of government is our unparalleled Civil Service. Our Civil Service is our glory and our pride. It is the admiration of all foreigners who see it, but it is—and I think I can appeal

THE DUTY OF PUBLIC SERVICE

to you, sir—it is much more the admiration of those who, as political Ministers, are called upon to witness its working from within. They constitute the wheels and the springs on which moves the great Juggernaut car of the State, and if these were once to get out of order, it would be an evil day indeed for Great Britain. But I confess, in my day dreams, I have sometimes wished to add to them one other department. I have sometimes wished that there was a department entirely devoted to training young men for the task of administration—men who would afterwards be ready to go anywhere and do anything at a moment's notice—be ready to go out and administer Uganda, for example, at a week's notice, ready to go and report anywhere on maladministration with the skill of an expert, able to investigate any subject and report upon it, not in the sense of Royal Commissions, but in a summary and a business-like manner. I should like them, as I say, to go at a word from their superior to any part of the Empire, and be able to do anything, as the militant orders of monasticism used to do—and do now, for aught I know—at the command of their superiors; to be, in fact, a sort of general staff of the Empire. I believe if that could be done it would be an incalculable gain; though I know it is a dream. But then I also know that it is not a bad thing sometimes to dream dreams. Of course, to some extent this function is performed by the Treasury. The Treasury, from its necessary contact with all the other departments, owing to its being alone able to furnish them with that financial staff of life without which they could not get on, a staff of life which can only—not always with a smile—be obtained from the Treasury, does furnish to the other departments men who are competent to do most things, and to undertake most duties. But that, unfortunately, has been already discovered. Already men have been constantly taken from the Treasury, and if that process be continued much longer that department will, I fear, be left in what I believe is scientifically called an anæmic condition. Well, gentlemen, I admit that this is a digression as well as a dream, but my point

THE DUTY OF PUBLIC SERVICE

is this, that there never was so great a demand as now for trained intelligence and trained character in our public service, and I should like to think that we of the Associated Societies will bear our part in it.

Most of you, I suppose, have already chosen the professions that you mean to pursue, and I should by no means wish to see, as the result of what I have said, a general exodus from Edinburgh to the somewhat forbidding portals of the Civil Service examiners. That is not my object, but I venture to point out that official duty is only a very small part of public duty, and that public work is by no means incompatible with other professions and other callings. I do not suppose I need remind you that Walter Scott was a sheriff, and that Robert Burns was an exciseman. But how often have I seen professional men clutch at an opportunity of serving their country, whether on a commission or on a committee, or something of that kind—clutch at it though knowing that it will involve a great waste of time, and therefore a great loss of money—clutch at it as an honour which they cannot sufficiently prize.

ADDRESSES

And I confess, when I see the enormous abilities that are given to our Civil Service and to our public service, either for no remuneration at all, or for remuneration incalculably smaller than the same abilities would have earned in any other calling or profession, I am inclined to think that the public spirit in this country was never higher nor brighter than it is at present. Let me tell you two curious stories which happened within my experience or knowledge with regard to this anxiety to serve the public. A friend of mine who had a high post in the Civil Service was asked, not so very long ago, to undertake some task which was peculiarly congenial to him, and for which he was peculiarly fitted; but he refused it without hesitation, and he gave as his reason this. He said, "When I was appointed to my present post at a very ample remuneration I knew nothing of the work, and it was some years before I could learn the work, to do it to my satisfaction. Now I have learned it, I am in a position in some way to repay the State for what it has done for me, and I shall not leave my post till

THE DUTY OF PUBLIC SERVICE

I feel I have in some degree discharged that debt." Well, now, a much longer time ago, before I can remember, there was one of the greatest and the wealthiest, and at the same time one of the most dissipated of the English nobility, who, after a life spent, as I say, in a very frivolous manner, was suddenly seized and bitten with the anxiety to occupy some public post under his Government and do some public work ; and he applied to the Minister of the day for some quite subordinate post, as he wished to do something to redeem his life. Well, the post was refused, and his life was unredeemed. I give that to you as a specimen, not so uncommon as it may seem, of the anxiety of men, who had not done much in their youth, as they approached middle life to be of some use to their country before they die. And, after all, gentlemen, we are bound to remember this—that we owe something to our country besides rates and taxes. Other countries have compulsory military service. We are released from that ; and if only on that consideration I think that we should be prepared to do something for the country which has done so much for us. And even if there is no public work ready to your hand, there are innumerable ways in which we can serve our country, however humbly and however indirectly. I only mention in passing the Volunteer movement. But there are social methods, literary methods, ay, and even athletic methods, because I am one of those who believe that one of the subordinate methods of welding the Empire together, and even of welding the English-speaking races together, is by those inter-colonial athletic contests, and athletic contests with the United States, which are developing so much in these days. But what I want to impress upon you is this, that if you keep before you the high motive of serving your country, it will ennoble the humblest acts that you do for her. The man who breaks stones on the road, after all, is serving his country in some way. He is making her roads better for her commerce and her traffic. And if a man asks himself sincerely and constantly the question—" What can I do, in however small a way, to serve my country?"—he will not be long in finding an answer.

THE DUTY OF PUBLIC SERVICE

Now, I will tell you what I consider the irreducible minimum of this service—the irreducible minimum. It is that you should keep a close and vigilant eye on public and municipal affairs; that you should form intelligent opinions upon them; that you should give help to the men who seem to you worthy of help, and oppose the men whom you think worthy of opposition and condemnation. That I believe to be the irreducible minimum of the debt of a British citizen to his country, and I believe it to be very important to the country. There is no such bad sign in a country as political abstention. I do not want you all to be militant politicians; I do not want it for your sake, or for the country's sake. But an intelligent interest does not mean a militant interest, though it, at any rate, means the reversal of apathy. We are told that there is a good deal of political apathy in these days. I do not know whether that is so or not, because I have no means of judging; but if there is political apathy, I think the cause of it is not far to seek. Our forefathers, with their defective news agencies or channels, were able to concentrate their mind on one particular subject at a time, and give it all their energy and all their zeal. For example, for some twenty years they were locked in that great war with Napoleon and the French Revolution, which absorbed all their energies, and when that war ceased there came an era of great single questions, on which they were able to concentrate all their attention. But now that is all changed. The telegraph brings you into communication with every quarter of the globe. Every day brings you news of some exciting character from every quarter of the universe, and under this constant and varying pressure the intelligence of men is apt to be dazed, and blunted, and dulled. And yet we know that when, as now, the attention of the country is concentrated on a single point, there is as little apathy as need be.

But I should not appeal even on these grounds to you, gentlemen, if I did not hold a somewhat higher and broader conception of the Empire than seems to be held in many quarters. If I regarded the Empire simply as a means of painting so much of the world red,

THE DUTY OF PUBLIC SERVICE

or as an emporium for trade, I should not ask you to work for it. The land hunger is apt to become land fever, and land fever is apt to breed land indigestion, while trade, however important and desirable in itself, can never be the sole foundation of an empire. Empires founded on trade alone must irresistibly crumble. But the Empire that is sacred to me is sacred for this reason, that I believe it to be the noblest example yet known to mankind of free, adaptable, just government. If that was only your or my opinion, it might perhaps be not very well worth having, but it derives singular confirmation from outside. When a community is in distress or under oppression, it always looks first to Great Britain; while in cases which are quite unsuspected, I think, by Great Britain at large, and which are, as a rule, only known to Ministers, they constantly express the wish in some form or other to be united to our country, and to enjoy our government. And, on the other hand, for the most part, in those territories which, for one reason or another, we have at various times ceded, we may, I think, in almost every case see signs of deterioration, and signs of regret on the part of the inhabitants for what they have lost.

I ask you then, gentlemen, to keep this motive before you of public duty and public service, for the sake of the Empire, and also on your own account. You will find it, I believe, the most ennobling human motive that can guide your actions. And while you will help the country by observing it, you will also help yourselves. Life in itself is but a poor thing at best ; it consists of only two certain parts, the beginning and the end—the birth and the grave. Between those two points lies the whole area of human choice and human opportunity. You may embellish and consecrate it if you will, or you may let it lie stagnant and dead. But if you choose the better part, I believe that nothing will give your life so high a complexion as to study to do something for your country. And with that inspiration I would ask you to blend some memory of this Edinburgh so sacred and so beautiful to us, not, perhaps, the Edinburgh of Cockburn or Jeffrey or Brougham, but an

THE DUTY OF PUBLIC SERVICE

Edinburgh yet full of noble men and wise teachers, that you will bear away some kindling memory of this old grey city, which, though it be not the capital of the Empire, is yet, in the sense of the sacrifices that it has made and the generations of men that it has given to the Empire, in the truest, the largest, and the highest sense an Imperial City.

OUR CIVIL SERVANTS

The Civil Servants are accustomed to hold a dinner every year; their Chairman in 1899 (on May 9th) was Lord Rosebery. This Address was his speech in proposing the toast of the evening, "The Civil Service." It will be noticed that in his opening sentences he refers to the preceding Address on "The Duty of Public Service."

OUR CIVIL SERVANTS

I HAVE taken on myself, in the despotic character of chairman, to put this toast (*The Civil Service*) before all the other services of the Queen. Sir Evelyn Wood rightly cheers, because this, to use the language of the last year of the nineteenth century, is the "show" of the Civil Service. The usual course of your chairman is to enter upon a long but a justified panegyric of all that the Civil Service does for the country. I do not propose to take that course, and I am glad to see that with the modesty inherent in the Civil Service that announcement is cheered. I do not do so for two reasons. In the first place, last autumn I had an opportunity of saying in Edinburgh what I thought of the Civil Service when there were no Civil servants there to blush. Now I should not care to see the whole audience turn crimson at hearing what I thought of them.

Another reason which debars me from praising you too much is that between me and the Civil Service there is a great gulf fixed. There is, of course, the obvious gulf which you think I meant—that you are in office, and that I am not. That is not what I mean, and I find it extremely necessary in these days to explain very clearly and explicitly what I do mean. The gulf that I speak of is this: that in our public offices there are two classes of officials. One is the political head, who, in the language of Lord Beaconsfield, may be described as a transient and embarrassed phantom who flits across the scene; and the other is a permanent official, who remains, and will remain while many Ministers cross his path. *Sedet aeternumque sedebit.* Well, as I belong to the first class, it is no use my pretending to praise the second too much. I think it better to keep up the description I have laid down, and speak as a more or less disinterested observer.

OUR CIVIL SERVANTS

But there is another difference between us. You know, I suppose, that ever since the time of Daniel, and I believe even as far back as the time of Pharaoh—I think my language recalls to you the worst moments of the examination that got you into the service—ever since the time of Daniel, and even back to the time of Pharaoh, there has been a broad distinction between those who make speeches and who dream dreams, and those who interpret them. I belong to the ingenuous class that makes speeches; you belong to the ingenious class that interprets them. And though I do not habitually dream dreams, I will venture to tell you a dream of mine, which you may interpret as you will. When I say that I make speeches, you may be well aware that I tell the truth; but when I say that you interpret them, you may think I am trading on your credulity. As a matter of fact I have hallucinations on the Civil Service, and one of them is this—that every morning the first object of a conscientious civil servant is to see the utterances of his political chief, to interpret them as best he can, and to trans-

ADDRESSES

mute them as well as he can into the work and the policy of his office.

Let me take a concrete example. On my right I see Sir Thomas Sanderson, with whom I have been more than once officially connected at the Foreign Office. I should be shocked if Sir Thomas Sanderson were to deny that when I was in office—I do not venture to speak of other Secretaries of State—the first thing he did in the morning, after opening the most urgent box of telegrams, was to set himself to read any speech that I might have made on the previous day—whether at a distribution of prizes to an athletic club, or at the opening of a library, and then to read into it what he had found in it, and secondly what he did not find in it, and, lastly, with an ultimate squeeze, what he could possibly derive from it by the unaided light of a boiling imagination; and I should be more annoyed if Sir Thomas Sanderson, refreshed by that intercourse with my intellect, did not proceed at once to apply to the foreign policy of the country the light he had derived from that almost inspired utterance. That is why

OUR CIVIL SERVANTS

I say that between the Civil Service and myself there is a great gulf fixed. But, after all, we all of us have our uses, and even a political phantom, who has ceased to be transient, and in that shape has ceased to haunt the public offices, may have an opinion founded upon what he has seen while he was in their midst.

I am not going to utter eulogies on the Civil Service, for the reasons I have stated, but I have occasionally been afflicted with dreams as to what would happen in certain conceivable circumstances, which may illustrate better than anything I can say what I think of the Civil Service.

Suppose that, as has happened in the other services of the Crown, there was to be a mutiny or a strike in the Civil Service. There was once a mutiny at the Nore. In the last century, Highland regiments, or at least one of them raised in the Highlands, declared that they would return to the Highlands. Suppose there was to be a strike of the Civil Service—the usual thing : an inadequate share of the profits, hours too long, the rules of the trade union transgressed—what would the country do? In those moments of the night when one sees those visions, I have attempted vaguely to conceive what would be the effect on the government of the country should there be such a strike. Of course we know the first outcome. From all the purlieus of Downing Street, and from all the recessess of Whitehall, there would come streaming forth in their hundreds of thousands first division clerks, and second division clerks, and all other mysterious categories, headed, I suppose, by men like Sir Edward Hamilton and Sir Francis Mowatt. They would proceed to Trafalgar Square and hold the customary meeting, the Under-Secretaries occupying the lions at the base of the Nelson monument. They would then go in a body to the House of Commons and present a monster petition, which would be allowed to lie in the courtyard of Westminster Palace. But in the meantime what would happen—what would become of the political heads? I have been a political head myself, and I view with a dismay and a despondency which I cannot express in words, what the position

OUR CIVIL SERVANTS

of a political head would be if he was deserted by his permanent subordinates. Of course his first business would be to import blacklegs into the office. From their various retreats you would see the retired civil servants, some of them covered with ribands, some adorned with coronets, and all, I hope, endowed with an adequate pension, brought back to the hated service of the State. You would telegraph for Sir Alfred Milner from the Cape of Good Hope. You would bring Lord Welby in chains from the chair of the County Council to occupy in that fettered condition his old armchair at the Treasury. And last, but not least, you would catch Lord Farrer. He is one of those men who acquire youth as they grow old, and my imagination of Lord Farrer as a blackleg in the Civil Service is this, that you would have to put him to look after half a dozen departments, which he would be able cheerfully to undertake, if, indeed, like the Duke of Wellington in 1834, he did not dispense quite adequately the whole business of Government.

Across this dream of mine there flitted one

spectral figure, which I could scarcely discern. I saw a shadow that seemed to be that of the Vice-President of the Council. The Vice-President of the Council is a transient political officer. But yet there is something permanent about him, too ; and what I could not understand, in the watches of the night, as I dreamt my dream, was this—whether the Vice-President of the Council threw in his lot with the permanent service to which, from some aspects of the case, he appears to belong, or whether he shared the nobler part of the political official, and dallied with Amaryllis in the shade—of course, I mean whether in some recess he was consulting with his noble friend the Lord President as to the exact doctrinal efficiency of some school catechism. Gentlemen, I suppose that such a strike as this would conclude as all strikes do. Some of the less venerable blacklegs might be treated with occasional contumely in the street. There would be a period of acute distress. The civil servants of the Crown would hold meetings for a considerable time; the political servants of the Crown would hold meetings for a considerable time; but at last there would be some *modus vivendi* found, and all would work happily again. But that fact is immaterial to me from my point of view, which is this, that during the time of the strike the work of the Government of the country would have sustained a blow of which no one who has not been in a public office, either in a political or permanent capacity, would have the faintest idea.

Now, I wish to say one word in a graver vein. I was reading the other day in a life of Sir Fitzjames Stephen what was said about the Civil Service by two successive Stephens. One was Sir James Stephen, the great Colonial Under Secretary, who said, when he was asked by a new civil servant what the position of a civil servant was, "You may write off the first joints of your fingers for them" —that is, the political officials, of whom I have been one in my time—" and then you may write off the second joints, and all they will say to you is, ' What a remarkably short-fingered man!'" Well, that, I think, represents a bygone view of the relations of the political heads to the permanent officials of the Civil Service. I do not believe that, however exacting or disagreeable a political head has been—and they have, I suppose, in moments of irritation or despondency, been both exacting and disagreeable—there has been lately any political head of a public office of whom you could believe such a thing as that. But Sir James Fitzjames Stephen, who was also connected with a public office, and who was in some sort for some time a permanent official, gave, I think, a juster view of the relations between the transient heads of offices and their permanent occupants. He said, " The understanding on which the permanent offices of the Civil Services of the Crown are held is that those who accept them shall give up all claim to permanent reputation on the one side, and be shielded from personal responsibility on the other." Well, I, as having been a political head, say most clearly and sincerely that we as political heads make a very good bargain if that statement is correct. The mistakes or the errors that we have to shield are remarkably few;

OUR CIVIL SERVANTS

the credit that we receive from the work of others in the permanent Civil Service is very great, and much more abundant than is usually supposed.

THE QUALITY OF JUDGMENT

The late Mr. Thomas Nelson—the well-known Edinburgh publisher—left £50,000 to provide four public libraries. The first of these, in the Fountain-bridge district of Edinburgh, was opened on May 10th, 1897, by Lord Rosebery, who, after obtaining entrance to the building with a silver key, spoke in public for the first time for several months. It will not be forgotten that a few months previously (in October 1896) he had resigned the Liberal leadership.

THE QUALITY OF JUDGMENT

I AM not sure that you, my Lord Provost, have not lured the humblest of your fellow citizens here under somewhat false pretences. You said this would be a small, informal sort of gathering, at which no serious speech would be expected of me, and then you make a sort of introductory series of remarks, in which you point out that this is not merely an occasion upon which a speech will be expected, but that it is the first of a long series of public speeches on public work for which, in your judgment, I am so eminently fitted. My lord, we will leave the entrancing subject of one's own personality, but I will only allude to it distantly for one moment more.

After a long and necessary silence there are one or two things which an audience has to

ADDRESSES

dread from the speaker who has been silent. In the first place, he may have altogether lost the capacity for speech. In the second place he may have stored up in him during the period of his reticence such overflowing masses of thought and matter, which he wishes to communicate to the first person he comes across, that his first audience may suffer under an avalanche of material. And the third and most fatal possibility of all is that he may combine both disabilities, that he may have lost altogether the faculty and capacity of intelligible speech, but may be at the same time overburdened and anxious to communicate illimitable thoughts to his fellow countrymen. I hope that I shall exemplify none of these three misfortunes to-day. I propose to say very little, because in opening public libraries I have said in my life most of what I wanted to say, and so I hinted to the Lord Provost on the occasion of that interview to which he has referred. But I could not refuse the invitation and indeed the pressure to come here on so interesting an occasion to open a building so full of possibilities—having opened,

THE QUALITY OF JUDGMENT

moreover, that central library of Edinburgh to which you, my lord, have alluded—and last and most especially to pay what tribute and honour my presence and my words could give to the memory of that wise and munificent citizen by whose legacy this building is erected. I understand that the central idea of this building, as you have set it forth, is this. In the first place, there is to be a recreation hall where, in the large and liberal phraseology of the testator, persons of the working classes can go to sit, write, read, converse, and otherwise occupy themselves; and, in the second place, that there is to be a free public library for this district united to this hall, and to supplement what this hall cannot always give. Now, there is this to be said about this connection which does not always fall to be said by those who open public libraries. As regards the connection of a club—because, after all, this is a club, only without ballot, without entrance fee, without subscription; it is a club for all the ordinary purposes of club life except that it will be open to all—I say that in this connection of a club and a free library one is

ADDRESSES

led to say one thing which does not always occur to those who open libraries alone.

What, ladies and gentlemen, is perhaps the most valuable and one of the most rare qualities which one meets with in the world? The quality of just and independent judgment. I suppose we all of us know in our various spheres of life the one invaluable friend we have, whose judgment we never doubt, whose advice we always follow, and to whose succour we have recourse whenever we are in doubt or in difficulty. That is the man of judgment whom we know well, and in the larger sphere of public life judgment is an even more precious, and, I should almost like to say in a whisper, not a less rare quality than in private life. Judgment is a possession of an enormous value to a nation, and in proportion as it contains men of judgment in direct proportion will that nation prosper. What is it that I mean by judgment in public affairs? I mean the capacity for taking a large, calm, and unbiased view. We are led by the hurry and the circumstances of life to take views which are neither large nor unbiased, nor detached

THE QUALITY OF JUDGMENT

from passion and from prejudice, and it is the quality of judgment which corrects those hasty and erroneous views. I wonder how many of all this nation of statesmen—because we are a nation of statesmen, or at any rate a nation of politicians, which is the next thing to being a nation of statesmen—I wonder, to qualify my first remark, which you received in disapproving silence, how many of this nation of politicians take the trouble or even have the opportunity to form a just judgment for themselves? Mouths have they, and speaking tongues have they, and utterance; but one sometimes wonders, when one sees the mouth work and the utterance come, whether one has not read something very like it in the paper that morning.

Well, of course, it is not the duty of newspapers to supply that large, leisurely judgment which I am endeavouring to impress upon you on this occasion as a necessity for a nation. They have to take the view of the moment, just as they have to give the news of the moment, and if they did and attempted more than this they would in some sense be some-

ADDRESSES

thing that was not a newspaper and be attempting something outside their province. The faculty of judgment, then, is, as it seems to me, to test these opinions as they come and go and to apply them to the touchstone of the faculty that I have called "judgment." No policy, just as no man, can be judged by the judgment of a week or of a day. A policy that can be considered in a day and judged in a day is no policy at all. Take the two most successful statesmen of our generation—but no, I suppose I should say of a former generation. When one has reached one's jubilee in life one does not make sufficient allowance for those who have the misfortune to be younger than oneself. Take the two most successful statesmen of the last half-century —Count Cavour and Prince Bismarck. If you had judged these men at certain periods, certain long periods, of their lives you would have been in danger of judging them and their policy unjustly. At one period one was called a madman, and at another period the other was called a traitor. But their policy required steadfastness, given by time alone, to

THE QUALITY OF JUDGMENT

enable it to operate and to be judged ; and where hasty judgment would have condemned it, a large, sober, reflective judgment has seen its results. I take that as an example, and I plead that, in an institution like this, the faculty of judgment may be obtained and cultivated. But where is it you obtain this inestimable quality ? You may obtain it as far as I know only in one of two ways ; but better in both — by intercourse with your fellow men and by reading. That is to say, by the intercourse with the minds of those who live around you, and by intercourse with the best minds of those who are dead. Well, this institution will supply both ; it will give you in this room the intercourse between man and man, without which all book learning is idle and fallacious, and on the other side it will give you the intercourse with the best minds that have existed in the world which is necessary to qualify the judgment of contemporaneous thought.

But it may also be said that you unite in this way an absolute union of conflicting interest, because, after all, if you read all that is given to you to read in the reading-room, you will not have much time to betake yourself to the library. One of the puzzles of the present day is how people find time to get through what they have to get through. What is the position of a man, for example, who tries, as many of my friends do, to read all the newspapers? There are many of my friends who feel that they cannot form a just opinion on all the events of the day until they read all the morning papers that are accessible to them. They rise early, they breakfast early, they begin immediately after breakfast to plod laboriously on through newspapers for hour after hour. And before their morning diet is complete there comes the whirl and rush of the evening papers, which occupy them until the evening meal. If they want to fill up the chinks they have the weekly papers, and then they have opposite them in a serried row the monthly magazines, and then if they aspire still higher, and have a crumb of time to spare, they have the good old quarterlies, which will take them their full time. I say this in itself is one of the great

THE QUALITY OF JUDGMENT

difficulties of the age. I do know men who spend their lives in this way. When they write their letters or take their recreation I do not know, and when they do their business I have no idea. But when they have completed this laborious reading of the periodical literature of the day accessible to them they proceed to the club and take all the newspapers published outside of their own domain. This makes a reading-room for newspapers a formidable competitor for the library, and where I think the greatest discrimination will be shown by those who are going to use these rooms and this library is as to where they will draw the line as to what is merely ephemeral and what is permanent and abiding in literature. I do not presume to offer advice on that point, but I desire to indicate that you in this building have two interests in reading which somewhat conflict with one another, and that it will not be very easy for those who frequent it to divide their time in such just proportions as to obtain the best results from both.

I do not know that I have much more to

add to these somewhat desultory remarks on the uses of the building we have come to open to-day. But I do not doubt that, whether it assists men in the invaluable faculty of forming a just judgment on affairs public and private or not, it will at any rate be an inexhaustible boon to the neighbourhood. It is one of the features of our age that in some way or another, partly through the working of the churches, partly through the working of perhaps a higher morality and a higher philosophy than was practised before, classes have drawn nearer to each other, men highly blessed and endowed with the worldly goods have desired to use their opportunities not so much in selfish gratification as in raising and bettering their fellow men. I believe that that is the best sign of our times. It is, I believe, more conspicuously seen in Great Britain than in any other part of the world, though in the United States we have some conspicuous specimens of benevolence. But as proof of this spirit I take our late fellow citizen. Mr. Nelson's bequest stands out conspicuously, and I know his wish was that

THE QUALITY OF JUDGMENT

this building, and the other buildings that may follow it if the experiment be successful, should not be of glowing architecture or such as to recall rather a monument to his memory than a delight to his fellow men. Yet I believe that is one of the sole provisions which he had in view that he will not be able to carry out, and that men as they pass this building, much less men as they use it, will bless that great citizen who thought of it, and provided for it before he passed away.

THE WORK OF PUBLIC LIBRARIES

On June 25th, 1896, Lora Rosebery opened a Free Public Library at Uxbridge Road, erected at the cost of Mr. Passmore Edwards in memory of Leigh Hunt and Charles Keene. The proposer of the vote of thanks to Lora Rosebery well described him as an "omnivorous reader."

THE WORK OF PUBLIC LIBRARIES

I THINK those who watch the growth of the free libraries system in this country, in spite of the almost persistent opposition of the ratepayers, have some cause to inquire, What object is it that these free libraries answer in our modern commonwealth? I confess I have formed a very clear conviction on that head. I think no one can watch the progress of our nation without seeing the enormous predominance that is given everywhere to-day to outdoor sports. I welcome that tendency. I think it is a healthy and rational tendency, but of course it may be carried too far. What we do see in the tendency to outdoor sport at this time is that it weans the race from occupations that might be objectionable, and it is rearing a noble and muscular set of human beings; and it subserves other objects which are not so immediately apparent. For instance, I take it the connection between Australia and the mother country has been rendered closer than it would have been otherwise by the cricket contests which take place between the two countries; and I am given to understand, though I have never seen one of the great northern or midland football matches, that they are almost Homeric in their character, in their strenuousness, and the excitement they engender. The rivalry they engender between the various districts of the country furnishes a subject healthy in itself and inspiring to all those who witness it. I hope very soon to see some such match, because I think we have lived in vain if we have not seen one. I have seen the crowds going to those matches, and I have never seen anything in public life or elsewhere comparable to the eagerness and the enthusiasm of those crowds. Then there is bicycling. I suppose nobody, not even the humblest pedestrian, with his arm broken or otherwise, is indifferent to the

WORK OF PUBLIC LIBRARIES

bicyclist. I do not know what particular effect the bicycle may have upon the conformation of posterity. It seems to me it may produce a race of beings of a Z-like shape. But, at any rate, it has produced a race of hardy adventurers such as those by whom our Empire was founded—adventurers perhaps a trifle too hardy, but who would have had no opportunity of visiting the corners of our native land if they had not been furnished with these useful wheels. All that is a most interesting and striking feature of our national life. We have to maintain a great Empire. We have to develop a great Empire, and for imperial purposes you need a race of muscle, of strength, and of nerve. All these are developed by these sports. But, after all, this is not everything. An empire cannot live by muscles alone. It must have brains. I suppose I shall be told at once that the brains are furnished by our educational appliances. I do not wish to undervalue our schools, either primary or secondary, or the work that the Universities have done inside or outside their limits. So large is my admiration that

ADDRESSES

I do not wish even to disparage the efforts of Governments in the cause of education.

But even education will not give you all that you want. What you want to develop in your race is the art of thinking, and thinking is an art which stands a very good chance of perishing from amongst us altogether. The risks to which independent thinking is exposed, when you come to reckon them up, are manifold and dangerous. I think the Press, with all its great merits, is one of the greatest enemies of independent thinking. To begin with, we are furnished every day from at least half a dozen quarters with the best thoughts of trained and able minds on the subject of the day in the daily papers. It is all that one able-bodied man can do to get through these able-bodied papers in the course of the day. Even if he feels inclined to think, and to correct the excellent thoughts which are thus supplied to him at a merely nominal figure by his own independent exercise of brain, he has not time to do it, and he becomes satisfied to become the walking reflex of the paper to which he happens to subscribe, or, what is more unfortunate still, of the many papers to which he subscribes, which may proproduce a confused habit of brain. Not merely have we that, but, if the appetite is sufficiently omnivorous, he has the weekly Press in profusion, with the more leisurely thoughts of distinguished minds, and if he has a minute or two left, he can read all the monthly magazines and complete the cycle of his intellectual system. But all this is bad for independent thought. We are grateful to those who supply those thoughts to us; but they ought not, in a properly constituted community, to supersede the thinking for ourselves. I am afraid that independent thinking is to some extent dying out among us. We have great waves of thought which do not so much arise in the community itself as among those who guide the community, and therefore—partly also, perhaps, from the quick succession of impressions that take place from the intercommunication of all parts of the world—the mind of England, which perhaps is the most receptive mind of the world, is becoming deadened and apathetic to external impressions. Now, I put one simple test to you. Take that melancholy shipwreck the other day. If you are asked about that shipwreck in a fortnight you will say, " Surely it did not take place so recently as that ; it must have taken place three months ago." Why is that ? Because of the number of impressions by which it has been constantly overlaid, and this great variety of impressions constantly stamped on the more or less receptive material of the brain gradually deadens impression and creates apathy, and I believe intellectual apathy is the great danger of our nation at this time.

That is the text from which I have to preach. I believe that this great work of public libraries is a great counter-irritant to that intellectual apathy ; I believe it furnishes an inducement to those who wish not merely to improve their bodies but their minds, who wish not merely to play but to think, who wish to have an opportunity or retirement from the first-hand impressions of the world and to form their impressions for themselves, to come to some temple of reading and of thought where they can form their conclusions

WORK OF PUBLIC LIBRARIES

and their convictions. Now, of course, it is a great deal to furnish the books and to furnish the house, but even that is not everything. I suspect that many people would say, on hearing that a free public library has been formed, "Oh, it will furnish nothing but a sort of gratuitous circulating library of all the sensational novels that come out." Well, a man had better read a sensational novel than read nothing; but I do not believe that is the experience of free public libraries. I do not believe they have simply furnished fiction to those for whom they cater. I believe the experience is that a fair proportion of thoughtful books are taken and digested—pre-eminently, I believe, by the artisan class.

But even then there is a difficulty. You take your man or woman or child, thirsting for knowledge, to those shelves. He longs to read something which will help him, and he does not know what he is to read, or how he is to get at the right book to read. Now, of course, many great geniuses have been formed or guided, as they have told us, by being left in a library quite free, and allowed to read whatever their mind guided them to, but I do not believe that to be a wholesome case at all. The number of books has increased so enormously, the titles, if I may say so, are sometimes so misleading, that a student who is thrown into a library under unrestricted conditions is apt to be very much like that confectioner's apprentice — I do not know whether he really exists or whether he is legendary—who on his first employment in a confectioner's shop is always allowed to eat as much as he chooses, in the sure confidence of his master that he will eat so much, and procure for himself so disagreeable an illness, that he will never wish to partake again. Well, I think that is the danger of the student who wanders into these libraries without any guide whatever to help him.

That brings me to my last point. I think every free public library requires a taster in the shape of a librarian—that is to say, a man who not only knows the outsides and the titles of books, but a man who knows the insides. They require a taster to guide the student as to what he wants. I do not know whether you have a taster in your librarian to-day, because I have only just made his acquaintance, but I do not doubt that you have. But it is a real and inestimable faculty. I believe that a tea-taster—a man who is endowed with the peculiar faculty of tasting tea and discriminating between the coarser and the finer kinds of tea—has a fortune in his palate; I believe that a man who can discriminate between the various kinds of silk by touch has a fortune in his fingers; but I am sure that neither of these is so valuable to the intellectual life of the nation as the taster who will guide the student to the books the student wants.

PARLIAMENTARY ORATORY

It is a favourite plan of Lord Rosebery's to say what he has to say after a lecture and not before it, and this address on "Oratory" was his contribution from the chair after Mr. Herbert Paul had given a lecture on the subject at Edinburgh on November 26th, 1896. The lecture was one of a series organised by the Edinburgh United Liberal Committee, but the occasion, if political, was so in form only.

PARLIAMENTARY ORATORY

The labourer is said to be worthy of his hire, but I am never quite sure why a vote of thanks is given to the chairman. Our assemblies are not so tumultuous as to require his intervention. He does not have, as in more favoured nations, to ring a bell, or even to put on his hat; and certainly I never felt myself so entirely over-paid as I do this evening. What I have done is to possess myself of the most comfortable chair in the room and to listen to one of the most brilliant and one of the most fascinating addresses that I have ever had the fortune to hear. I owe Mr. Paul a debt for that lecture, and if Mr. Shaw had not already moved a vote of thanks to him I should move another; and I have a special reason for thanking him which Mr.

ADDRESSES

Shaw had not, and it is this—that when, owing to recent interesting events, I thought it best to cancel my political engagements, Mr. Paul, who had chosen a political topic for his lecture, kindly changed it at very short notice so as to make this a non-political engagement and evade my self-denying ordinance. Now, on the other hand, we must always be fair, and I have one slight cause of complaint against my friend. I hoped when I heard the topic on which he proposed to address us that I should receive some practical hints as to the best method of making a speech. I knew I should go away refreshed, but I hoped I should go away improved. Now I do not think that he has given us any practical hints, except that we are not to overstate our case, and that we are not to write our speeches.

I do not think he furnished any very cogent argument against writing one's speech, because he truly said that those who resort to that practice have the happy faculty of inserting into their speech beforehand the enthusiasm which it is sure to evoke, and to procure

PARLIAMENTARY ORATORY

ready-made for their witticisms the laughter that they ought to elicit, but he left out by far the most important disadvantage which attends that method of oratory, and it is this —that sometimes, when you have sent your speech to the papers and it has been printed and published, you have not had an opportunity of actually delivering it. That has happened on more than one occasion, and it has been a damper to an otherwise unexceptionable practice. Now, there are one or two marginal notes, if I may so say, that I might venture to make on what Mr. Paul has said. I think he went too far, if he will allow me to say so, unless my recollection is quite wrong, in saying that you can read the speeches of Pitt and Fox almost as they were delivered. My reason for saying so is this. Pitt, I think, corrected only two of his speeches for publication, and of one of those speeches he wrote—for I have seen the letter—that the report was so hopelessly incorrect that when he began to correct it he had to re-write it. I think that that in itself is a sufficient instance that Mr. Paul went too far in his assertion,

ADDRESSES

and I think also that if you read the records of the Parliamentary debates of that time you will feel assured that the reports were not extraordinarily accurate.

Then there is another note I would make. Mr. Paul attributed to Mr. Gladstone the saying that if a speech read well it must be a bad speech. Mr. Gladstone may have said it, but the person who first said it was Mr. Fox. Somebody said to Mr. Fox, "Have you read So-and-so's speech? It is an excellent speech." "Does it read well?" said Mr. Fox; "because be sure if it does it is a very bad speech." Now, Mr. Paul may say that Mr. Gladstone may have made that remark in those words, but I will bring forward again, as in the case of Mr. Pitt, my indirect proof—that Mr. Fox said not "very" but a word beginning with "d"; and I am sure you will agree with me that that puts Mr. Gladstone's having said it out of the category of human possibilities.

Let me make a short marginal note, not in the way of correction this time, but in the way of supplement. Mr. Paul alluded to that most remarkable speech of Mr. Gladstone on moving the vote of credit in 1885 in which he procured eleven millions sterling without a single speech being made in reply. I think that is one of the most remarkable achievements recorded in the House of Commons. I think it is one of the most important—I doubt if any speech, not merely by its magnificence, but by the fact of its being followed by a unanimous vote, ever produced such an effect on the continent of Europe. It had an effect wholly for good and wholly for peace. The fact of its being absolutely unopposed—the fact of this happy result, I would rather say—was due to some extent to an accident. Lord Randolph Churchill, who then led the Fourth Party, was away, taking a little refreshment. It was dinner-time when Mr. Gladstone ended—it was not wholly unnatural—and while Lord Randolph was at dinner Mr. Gladstone sat down and the debate collapsed. Lord Randolph always complained bitterly that the debate had not been maintained, and said that he should certainly have entered the lists, and I do not think we need doubt he would have entered the lists if he had been in the House;

but that is an incidental circumstance—a very happy circumstance, I think, but an incidental one. But a still more curious incident followed that speech, as showing the effect or the transient effect of Parliamentary oratory. Within six weeks of that speech being delivered and that unanimous effect being produced the Government was turned out of office. I do not know what moral to draw from that. It is perhaps a painful one if it be drawn at all, but as a member of that Government I remember the circumstance very clearly, and I rather regret that Mr. Paul should not have mentioned it and drawn the moral which I myself am unable to do.

I could add another instance, but not so solid a one, to the influence of a speech over votes. It was in the House of Lords when the Liberal Government was in, and a great Government measure was brought up before the House of Lords, and two peers of my acquaintance, who belonged to the Opposition, came down to the House determined, in spite of their being Tories, to vote for it. But a leading member of the Government rose and

PARLIAMENTARY ORATORY

delivered from the Treasury bench so powerful a speech in its advocacy that when he sat down my two friends determined to vote against the Bill. That is not a very satisfactory way of turning votes, but that is the only solid concrete instance that I can tell of in which in the House of Lords a speech has influenced votes —at least it is the only one that I can call to mind. Mr. Paul left out perhaps a historical instance before Mr. Gladstone's time of speeches influencing votes. It was when, if you remember, Lord Macaulay—of course, he was a member for Edinburgh, as most eminent men have been at some time of their lives—when Lord Macaulay, on a question of allowing the Master of the Rolls to keep his seat in the House of Commons, turned the House of Commons completely round in his favour, and enabled that judge, by an exception which we can now hardly understand, to retain his seat in that House. After all, is not this the real practical importance of Parliamentary eloquence? We talk of Parliamentary eloquence as if it was an ornamental study to be pursued for its own sake,

ADDRESSES

and we are apt, I think, a little to forget that the object and sole end of Parliamentary eloquence is to persuade for what you believe to be a good cause. I suppose there is one great instance of that, to whom Mr. Paul only alluded passingly this evening because he was not a great orator. Yet he was the most effective orator of his time—I mean Mr. Cobden. Mr. Cobden sat down after one of Mr. Bright's great speeches and said with friendly frankness—a frankness that nobody but Mr. Cobden would have used—"Gentlemen, I do not deal in perorations." But the effect of his speech was narrated in those words which Mr. Paul has quoted from Bright's speech at Bradford.

Let me take another wonderful instance—it comes very near home to you—in which oratory, outside Parliament entirely, brought about a great change in this country : I mean what is known as the Mid Lothian campaign. Lord Beaconsfield then had a very strong Government. When the general election came he chose to adopt a policy of silence. He wrote, if I remember rightly, only a short letter to

PARLIAMENTARY ORATORY

the Duke of Marlborough as an appeal to the electors. Mr. Gladstone, on the other side, assumed a directly contrary policy, and nobody can doubt that one cause by which an enormous Parliamentary majority was pulled down at that election and an enormous Parliamentary majority on the other side was built up was due wholly and entirely—so far as wholly and entirely can be applied to a general election and its causes—to the oratory of Mr. Gladstone on that occasion.

On the other hand, in the United States we have just seen an opposite result. The victorious candidate for the Presidency shrouded himself in silence, and we are calculating by the hundreds and the thousands and the millions the number of words that the defeated candidate uttered in the course of his campaign. You cannot always, then, draw an inference even from that; but my point is this, that Parliamentary eloquence, whether it be exalted or whether it be merely plain and forcible, is only of the slightest value so long as it is used as a weapon in the cause that the user believes to be good. You may think that a platitude, but there is nothing less a platitude than that.

What flatterer of Parliamentary institutions can say that the speeches in Parliament are dictated solely by the wish to convert their hearers to a good cause? Have we heard of nothing in the shape of speeches intended merely for delay? And I am sure that in all those full-dress debates which are supposed to be necessary to the second reading of an important Bill, from the heavy artillery of the front benches, which deals such tremendous death and destruction, to the humbler squibs that come from the back or the side benches, there is much that might be left out if argument and persuasion were solely the object at heart. Do we not a little forget in these days that Parliament itself is not an end and an object, but only a method and a means? Parliament exists, not as an arena in which great men or small men or mediocre men may deliver long speeches, but to further the highest interests of the nation, to secure the free expression of the wishes of the nation, and to guarantee the good government of the nation

PARLIAMENTARY ORATORY

to pass wise and just laws, and to see that due consideration is given them. What Parliament has not always seen is that undue consideration is sometimes given. I sometimes believe, I sometimes bring myself to think, that some of those who are swaddled and brought up in Parliament and who spend long periods of life in Parliament are apt to forget this great elementary truth, and that they would not mind a Session which was absolutely barren of results as long as the speeches had been good and copious, and as long as the debating had remained at the high standard of the best traditions of the House of Commons. Surely that is all wrong. I do not say we do not want better Parliamentary oratory, but we want a good deal less of it. If we could attain the standard to which Mr. Paul calls our attention we should not deem oratory always a waste of time. But to have Parliamentary time—so precious for many purposes—devoured by the speeches which have so little to recommend them except their length is a trial of patience to the lovers of all free institutions. You have not

ADDRESSES

mentioned the speaker of whom I sometimes think with the fondest admiration of all. Sir Joshua Reynolds ended his addresses at the Royal Academy by saying that he wished to end his discourses with the name of Michael Angelo. I, if I want a sentence to sit down on, will sit down on this—that I regard with honour, with admiration, and with constant envy, the memory of single-speech Hamilton.

THE ENGLISH-SPEAKING
BROTHERHOOD

On July 7th, 1898, Dr. Charles Waldstein gave a Lecture at the Imperial Institute on "The English-speaking Brotherhood." Lord Rosebery was in the chair, and this Address is his after-lecture commentary. The lecturer pleaded for " English-speaking" as against " Anglo-Saxon," urging that the unsound ideas respecting our racial origin involved in the expression " Anglo-Saxon" would do more harm than good to the cause of a better understanding between Great Britain and the United States. But it will be noticed that "Anglo-Saxon" found in Lord Rosebery, if not a supporter, at least an apologist.

THE ENGLISH-SPEAKING BROTHERHOOD

I AM sure I am only expressing your views when I tender, on your behalf, our thanks to Professor Waldstein for the extremely interesting address he has delivered to us this afternoon. He has set forth with a fulness and eloquence, and a learning which leaves nothing to be desired, his views on a question which is, perhaps, of the most vital interest to the English-speaking brotherhood—to use his own expression—of any that can lie before them. And, although I may not agree in detail with all his views and with all that he has laid down, and it would, perhaps, be impossible for any two human beings to agree to so many propositions as he has laid down in the course of his speech, I think we may come to the general conclusion with him that, under whatever name we may choose to call it, or whatever form it may assume, the good understanding, the more cordial the better, between the—I hardly know what to call it, for I may not use the word Anglo-Saxon—the British and American races is one fraught with benefit to the best destinies of mankind.

But I must warn you against a pitfall that lurks even in that expression. It is this—that, putting aside the conscientious Russian, whom the Professor summoned to give testimony, I am afraid all the other great nations of the world are under the same impression as to the spread of their power and their empire. I doubt if the Germans or the French, for example, and I make bold to say even the Russians, though they have been quoted against the argument by the lecturer, would be disposed to say that the extension of their several empires was not in the best interests of the human race. That is a feeling common to all nationalities, and we can only hope that we indulge in it with more

ENGLISH-SPEAKING BROTHERHOOD

reason and on a broader basis than do the others I have mentioned.

Our lecturer took exception to the term Anglo-Saxon, and he took exception very justly to that term as not being truly a scientific description of our race. But I think he would agree with me in saying that the same objections would lie against a generic description of almost any other race in the world—that there is hardly a race in the world inhabiting its own territory—I cannot recall one at this moment—which can be strictly called a race, if all the objections which lie against the term Anglo-Saxon lie against the adjective which may be applied to that race. I do not plead for the word Anglo-Saxon. I would welcome any other term than Anglo-Saxon which in a more conciliatory, a more scientific, and more adequate manner would describe the thing I want to describe. But whether you call it British or Anglo-Saxon, or whatever you call it, the fact is that the race is there and the sympathy of the race is there. How you arrive at that sympathy, whether it be purely by language, or as, perhaps, I think more truly, by the moral, intellectual, and political influences under which a nationality has grown up—how you arrive at that sympathy, it is foreign to my purpose to discuss to-day. But this at least we may say, that when a nation has inhabited certain boundaries without disturbance for a considerable number of centuries, even though it has received accessions from foreign nations, and when it has fused those accessions from foreign nations into its own nationality, and made them accept the name and language and laws and the facts of that nationality, it seems to me that for all practical purposes you have a nation and a race.

Is not that the case with ourselves and the United States? Up to July 4, 1776, we lived under the same Constitution, with the little divergences which Great Britain permits to her external dependencies all over the world. Then came the great crash of July 4 and the treaty of 1783. I suspect that to those who lived in those days it appeared that the sun of England had set. It was so expressed by her greatest statesman. It was felt to be a

ENGLISH-SPEAKING BROTHERHOOD

blow from which she could never recover. George III., though we may not agree with him in many things, felt that from the bottom of his soul, and he would not sign any acknowledgment of American independence until it was wrung from him by the sternest necessities. But history moves on. Do we not now recognise that that Declaration of Independence and acknowledgment of independence was not merely a good thing for the development of the United States, but also a good thing for the development of Great Britain? If those nations were ever to become close friends, as there seems some prospect of their becoming now, it was an almost indispensable precedent in the conditions at which they had arrived that the United States should become an independent body of States; and we, on the other hand, can feel this, that if we had remained connected with the United States as we were before we should probably have been satisfied and engrossed with the management of that great empire and should not have sought the infinite accretions which have come to our

ADDRESSES

Empire since that date and rendered it worldwide even without the United States. Therefore, on both sides we have profited. If there is to be a common bond the United States comes into it infinitely greater and stronger than it would have been if it had lived under our dominion, and we on our side bring to the common stock a far greater and wider empire than would be the case if we had remained united.

This is a very practical question. It is not merely a question for perorations, but it is a question of the most vital and practical politics. We see the Old World, the old continental world, gradually moulding itself into an attitude of not unmixed friendliness to the race which I must not name. After all, that was to be expected. So long as we were left free to develop our colonial ambition without any particular concurrence there was no conflict of interest which would lead us into any violent antagonism to the older empires of the earth. But now almost all these empires have developed a colonial policy of their own, and therefore it was hardly possible under

ENGLISH-SPEAKING BROTHERHOOD

these conditions that a position of extreme friendliness should continue to exist between those who were seeking colonial empires and that which already possesses one. You must not perhaps blame the European States for their attitude towards us. It is much wiser to explain it by natural reasons. But whether it be a wise attitude towards us or not, we have all to recognise, to whatever party in the State we may belong, that it is an attitude which has to be reckoned with, and that in future we must not rely too much on the extreme and altruistic friendship of some European States on which we had reckoned, and must be prepared to hold our own—I do not mean necessarily by warfare—but to hold our own in the great struggle for the division of the world which seems to be immediately impending over us.

How very little of the world in a very short time there will remain to divide! Has anybody taken that very seriously to heart? Africa is portioned out into spheres of influence of more or less value. Asia is being portioned out with a rapidity to which all previous partitions must yield the palm. There is practically nothing else left in the world to divide, and you will presently arrive at this—the world mapped out into several great portions, several great predominating influences, not necessarily actually hostile to each other, but commercially not likely to be very friendly. That points, I think, to the fact that the next war—the next great war, if it ever takes place—will be a war for trade and not for territory. Therefore, in looking round for the interest which most coincides with ours, even putting apart the question of nationality, we look naturally to the United States, which, though it has a protective tariff, is internally a great free-trade continent, and which certainly has no wish to see the external ports of the world closed to her commerce. The United States claims, and not without justice, that though she has a tariff which shuts out many European importations, yet so vast is the continent within her tariff, so great is the number of the population of the States over which she presides, and among which there is free trade, that she is practically a free-trade collection of States in the best meaning of the word. If that is so—if race and commerce, if the sympathies that arise from common nationality, the influence of centuries, the influence of intellectual training and political tradition are all ranged on one side in our connection with the United States—it is not necessary, as it seems to me, and still less would it be expedient, to draw any formal bond which should define those relations and those sympathies. But this, I think, at least we may say—whatever the foundation may be, whether it be one of race, or religion, or language, or interest, the moment is coming when, to use the sublime words of Canning, we may once more call the New World into existence in order to redress the balance of the Old.

SCOTTISH HISTORY

This Address on Scottish History was delivered on November 23rd, 1897, in Dowell's Rooms, Edinburgh, when Lord Rosebery, as President, took the chair at the Annual Meeting of the Scottish History Society.

SCOTTISH HISTORY

WHAT is the prospect that the report holds out to us as regards publication? In the first place, we have the books for next year; "The Papers Relating to the Scots Brigade," at the Hague, which is a subject of singular and original interest, which, I am sure, we shall welcome. Then there comes the "Montreuil Correspondence," which will throw light on what, I think, all will acknowledge to be a very obscure part of Scottish history, and which will furnish invaluable material to the historian. Then we have "The Accompt Book of Wedderburn" during the end of the sixteenth and part of the seventeenth century, which, I think, falls closely within the scope of what we had in view when we founded the society, to throw light on the life of the country and the people, and I am sure nothing can do that so much as the Scottish accompt books which we have been privileged to inspect and to publish. But, if I may say so, the *bonne bouche*, in my opinion, of all that is held out to us is " The Memorials of John Murray of Broughton." We all remember the famous story of Sir Walter Scott's father and the mysterious stranger who partook of tea in Sir Walter Scott's father's house, and the father Scott throwing the tea-cup out of the window and saying, " Neither lip of me or mine comes after Mr. Murray of Broughton's." That is a singular and sinister incident, and the memory of Murray of Broughton is not altogether savoury in the nostrils of history, but, for all that, that only makes the publication of his own *apologia* the more interesting. I have been privileged, owing, I suppose, to my official position, to have a private taste of this publication, and I can assure you that your anticipations will not be disappointed, and that you will not regret the delay which has enabled Mr. Fitz-

SCOTTISH HISTORY

roy Bell to add a considerable number of original papers from the Record Office and from Her Majesty's collection at Windsor to that book. The only part I have not seen of the book is perhaps that which we shall all like the best, which is the introduction by Mr. Fitzroy Bell. But that is a part which cannot be hurried, and I am assured it is in good progress, and it will make the volume additionally welcome when it comes.

Will you forgive me if I say one or two words on the general scope and work of our society? In doing so, I feel rather reminded of the speech by the late genial Sir George Harvey, the President of the Royal Scottish Academy, which I heard him make at one of the banquets of the Academy, which have, unfortunately, fallen into abeyance. Sir George Harvey was delighted with the exhibition, and he made a speech which amounted in brief to this: there never was such an Academy and there never were such pictures. Well, that is my view of our society. I shall express it quite frankly; there never were such publications.

ADDRESSES

I very much doubt if any one can find any serious fault with anything that the society has done or with any publication that the society has put forward, and I venture to ask you of what other society known to you can so much be said? What is it we have been privileged to do? What is the gap that we have been enabled to fill up? I think all our publications are valuable. I am sure they are. But some epochs and some subjects appeal more especially to some than to others, and I think that we may say that on two subjects of great importance we have been enabled to do a good work—work which perhaps no other society could have done. Besides that, I flatter myself—but here I cannot carry my contention into the region of proof—that we have done much more than simply instruct by our publications. We have done something in the way of inspiration to writers, and of inducing many to tread the field of Scottish history who might not have been so attracted except by our publications. I will take one book, the author of which is personally unknown to me, and which I have read and

SCOTTISH HISTORY

which I dare say you have read with the greatest admiration and delight. "The Byeways of Scottish History," by Mr. Henry Colville of Glasgow. I cannot say for certain —for I have absolutely no knowledge on the point—that that book has derived any inspiration from our work, but I like to think that it has.

What, then, are the two subjects on which I think it has been the privilege of this society to do the most important work? The first is the history of the Stuart family after the abdication of James II., and that is a period of history which is still open to the historian. The history of the Stuarts after the abdication of James II., in spite of the invaluable material that exists both at Windsor and elsewhere, and in spite of the very valuable monographs on the various rebellions which they inspire, remains yet, I think, to be properly put in shape. Now, we have done a good deal in that way. I myself have been privileged to co-operate by the publication of some lists of those who took part in the rebellion of '45. I do not mention that fact as an encouragement to others, but I mention it because of the warning it gave to me, which will last me as long as my life. In a preface to that book I put in an extract, which I duly copied from a veracious authority, but when I was challenged as to my authority I have never been able to put my hand on it from that day to this or to find the pamphlet from which I extracted it. Therefore, it is only one more confirmation of the invaluable advice given by an aged sage to one who sought his guidance in life, "Always wind up your watch at night, and verify your quotations." But I also like to think that, if I have not been able to do very much myself, I made a suggestion at the last meeting I was able to attend which bore instant fruit. I do not believe the result was due to my suggestion—I am not so vain as to think so—but I am happy to think that two minds came together and the result was that the suggestion I made—that we might have an itinerary of the wanderings of Charles Edward after the battle of Culloden—has borne fruit, and has been admirably carried out by Mr. Blaikie in a volume which is now published. Now, let me make another suggestion, which I hope will be equally fruitful. Before the history of the Stuarts can be written there is a book which must be compiled and will not be easily compiled. I suppose you all know Haydn's "Book of Dignities," which has been continued in a later edition by a Mr. Ockerby, and published by Messrs. Allen and Sons. It contains all the prominent honours and dignities and Ministries which have been conferred by the Monarchy during the whole period of our history, but what is wanted is a book of those dignities which were conferred by the Stuarts after their departure from England in 1689. During almost all that time they had their Secretaryships of State, and their peerages, their knighthoods and their various dignities, and a list of that kind would be a most valuable assistance to an historian of the Stuarts. I quite admit that the first edition might not be a very complete book, because I say there would be some difficulty in the compilation, but the first edition would bring out so many suggestions and put the editor

ADDRESSES

on the track of so many papers that the second and the third and fourth editions would be works of incalculable value to historians.

Now I daresay you might say, What is the use of any such book? The dignities died with the people, and they were not of much interest when they existed. But that is not the fact. Historians, with all respect be it said, are not sufficiently careful in matters of detail. They do not give us the actual date of resignations of power and accessions to power, and in the majority of histories, if anybody wishes to read them accurately, they have to read them with some sort of calendar of dignities with the exact dates by their side and with the book which I suggest. There is also this to be said, that whereas dignities and Ministries are, perhaps, of ephemeral interest when conferred by dynasties that are actually existing, there is an element of sympathetic pathos about them when they represent nothing but a faded, an abdicated, and a banished power. I am not sure that the whole calendar of the melancholy Court of the Stuarts, their shadowy Secretaries of State, and their purely nominal dignities would not have a greater interest both for the historian and the student of human nature than that book of Haydn's to which I have referred, which tells you of those who enjoyed power and substantial rank.

I pass from that subject—the history of the Stuarts—where, I am sure, we have laid a sure foundation for the future historian, and I come to another subject of which a history has also to be written, and where, I think, we shall some day be recognised as having done an incalculably good work—I mean the history of Scotland in the eighteenth century. The history of Scotland in the eighteenth century has, I think, by all avowal, never been written. You have had the history of the two or three rebellions that were stirred up by the Stuarts or by their agents. You have had copious histories of the Union. You have had the history of the Porteous mob told in great detail and by a great master of fiction as well. You have had the Darien scheme told in great detail. Wherever

ADDRESSES

the history of Scotland in the eighteenth century has touched politics it has been told, but the history of Scotland in the eighteenth century only in a very rare and indirect degree did touch politics at all. After the Union, I think we may say that Scotland determined to take, with the disability of the loss of her separate government, the full advantage of it. She gave herself up to fitting herself for the great part that she was destined to play in the government of the British Empire. She recovered by a long period of repose the exhaustion of the political part of her history, which was all excitement and which was no repose ; and as the affluent forces of nature gather themselves together under the uniform and impassive covering of the snow, so under the apparent deadness and moderatism of the eighteenth century Scotland was collecting her strength for the effort which she has put forward in the nineteenth. But there is even more to be said than this. She gained not merely by her reserve and recuperation of strength in the eighteenth century, but by the removal of the Court and of the Parliament and of the fashion of Scotland to the southern metropolis, she was enabled to develop in her rural districts types of independent character which I am sorry to say, under the influence of the more successful nineteenth century, with its railways and its hurry and its newspapers, are rapidly disappearing, and which it will be the privilege of the historian of the eighteenth century carefully to recall.

I have been much longer than I intended to be, but I was anxious to call attention to the two fields in which I think we have done specially valuable work, and which, I think, may encourage the historian of the future. I think the historian of the eighteenth century will not be able, perhaps, to confine his researches to that century. He will have to carry it on to the first quarter of the nineteenth, for the period of which I speak hardly ceased till the Ministry of Mr. Canning, and indeed, some of us have been able to see in our lifetime survivals of these rare types of lairds and of divines, and of the servants of divines, which are specially racy and character-

ADDRESSES

istic of the Scottish nation and of Scottish soil. As long as we do this good work I wish more power to our arm ; in fact, as long as the Scottish History Society exists I look forward with a certain confidence to the future. Of the history of the present we know nothing whatever. In despite of the invaluable agencies which report to us almost every event as soon as it occurs, we can only learn partially and imperfectly the real story of our times. What we get from day to day is, as it were, a kodak view, limited, narrow, and piercing, but so limited that for the purpose of history it is of little value. It will be a century hence before the large and serene gaze of history can focus itself sufficiently on the events of the day to be able to place them in their true relation and their true proportion, and I trust and firmly believe that a hundred years hence the Scottish History Society will be still active and vigorous, and perhaps pointing its focus towards the somewhat distracting and distorted events of the age in which we live.

ETON

On October 28th, 1898, there was a great gathering of Old Etonians (never slow to celebrate their own good fortune) at the Café Monico, to say "good-bye" and wish "good luck" to the Earl of Minto, Governor-General of Canada, Lord Curzon of Kedleston, Viceroy of India, and the Rev. J. E. C. Welldon, Bishop of Calcutta. Lord Rosebery, as a distinguished Old Etonian, was in the chair, and proposed the toast of " Our Guests" in the speech which is here printed.

ETON

THIS is, I think, in some respects the most remarkable dinner at which I have had the honour of assisting. So brilliant is the gathering that I would almost seem to require a pair of smoked glasses to contemplate the various dazzling celebrities who owe their various successes to Eton, and who are assembled round this table. And I should be for my part extremely uneasy at my position in the chair were it not that I well understand that, on an occasion like this, the best service a chairman can render is to say as little as possible and to obliterate himself. I remember a story that the late Lord Granville used to tell me—for dinners to outgoing Viceroys and Governors had not been hitherto unknown —they were habitual. Lord Granville was a

ADDRESSES

guest at a dinner to an outgoing Governor of very indifferent powers of speaking, and as the Governor-designate laboured through his speech Lord Granville in sheer weariness cast his eye on the notes of the speech that lay before him and saw marked in red ink, copiously underlined, the words "Here dilate on the cotton trade." I forget the end of the story, but with a man of Lord Granville's readiness of resource it is not difficult to surmise that those notes disappeared on the instant and that the orator very soon followed their example. I shall not be guilty to-night, and I trust that the numerous Viceroys who bristle around me and who are announced to speak will not either, of dilating on the cotton trade, and I think that that is a course that will meet with your approbation.

But there is another reason that makes it impossible to speak long on this occasion. There is a theory, well known to the Foreign Office, that every ship of war is, wherever it may be found, the territory of the country to which it belongs, and on that hypothesis I

ETON

hold that this apartment, which bears all the characteristics of a London coffee-room of the most refined and brilliant kind, is, after all, Eton territory—is Eton; and no one who has had experience of the debates of Parliament, or even of the conversations of Etonians when we were Etonians, will think for a moment otherwise than that brevity is the soul of wit. The words "rot" and "bosh" would have been applied—not, perhaps, improperly—to any one who exceeded the limits of perhaps three or four minutes. This leads me into a vein of thought which is not without its complications. If this is Eton territory, one at most feels as if the celebration should be essentially Etonian in more ways than one, and I seem to see, through a glass darkly, the vision of our Viceroys and Bishop-designate drinking "long glass" as part of their initiation. On the present occasion there is no "long glass" present, or I am sure that I should receive your support in moving that that ceremony should be undergone.

Yet, after all, there are circumstances in

this gathering that are not so hilarious. It is pretty clear that we are all of us a long way from Eton, a long way from " bosh," a long way from " rot," and the other associations that I have endeavoured to recall. We are not, indeed, without connections with Eton. We are honoured to-night with the presence of the Provost and the Headmaster ; but otherwise our associations with Eton are getting somewhat dim and distant. They are represented chiefly by the presence of our relations in the first, second, and third generation who are privileged to be pupils within its walls, and I am not sure that there is not an intensified feeling of gloom at finding that you have among your juniors at Eton a Viceroy of India and a Bishop of Calcutta going forth in the full maturity of their powers to discharge those important functions. But, after all, that is a fate that had to come to all of us at some time or another. We had to draw a lengthening chain, lengthening daily as regards our connection with Eton. We must be prepared to see our successors grow up, and we must—it sounds trite to say so—be prepared to feel a little older every day. But there is one consolation in getting older as an Etonian—that you keep the pride that has always been in you since you went to Eton, the pride of the prowess of your school. I never knew but one Etonian who said he did not like Eton, and he very soon went to the devil. At any rate, whether we are privileged to be Viceroys or Bishops, or have to lead a life of greater obscurity, we at any rate may glory in this—that we belong to the school that with an everlasting current of eternal flow turns out the Viceroys and the Bishops and the Ministers of the Empire that the Empire requires.

The Duke of Wellington said—and I am sure you will expect this quotation—that in the playing-fields of Eton—he did not know how far they were to extend, what deserts they were to encompass—the battle of Waterloo was won. But a great deal more than the battle of Waterloo has been won in the playing-fields of Eton, and that somewhat presumptuous list that is printed on the back of our bill of fare calls to

ADDRESSES

mind how in at least two great dependencies of the Empire—the Indian Empire and, if I may so call it, the Canadian Empire—Eton has played a conspicuous part. What, for example, would Canada have done without Eton, when out of the last six Viceroys all but one are Etonians? And although my friend Lord Aberdeen is an unhappy exception, I do not doubt but if he could have been he would have been an Etonian. Is there not something pathetic to us in our Alma Mater going on turning out the men who govern the Empire almost, as it were, unconsciously? But, although I speak in the presence of the Provost, of the Headmaster, of Mr. Durnford, of Mr. Ainger, of Mr. Marindin, and of other great guides of Etonian thought, they will not, I think, dispute the proposition when I say that, however great the learning that Etonians take from Eton may be, the highest and the best part of their education is not the education of the brain, but the education of the character. It is character that has made the Empire what it is and the rulers of the Empire what they are. I will not dilate longer on this theme. I wish only to play a slightly conspicuous part on this occasion, and, after all, if we were once to begin to dilate on the merits and the glories of Eton we should not separate to-night. There is another reason that appeals to me to curtail these remarks.

One of our distinguished guests, though he was born and nurtured and trained at Eton, has up to very lately occupied the position of headmaster of an establishment which I perhaps ought not to name on this occasion, but which I am sorry to say is painfully present to our minds about the middle of July. I have no doubt Mr. Welldon's Etonian experience has moulded Harrow into something more like Eton than it used to be. Of course, of that I have no personal experience or knowledge; but this I do know, that, making a great sacrifice, as men call sacrifice, in position and perhaps prestige, giving up one of the most envied of all English positions, he is going out to take the Bishopric of Calcutta under circumstances which must commend him to all his brother Etonians. He is going to fill the See of Heber, animated, as I believe, by the principles of that noble hymn which Heber wrote, and I firmly believe that one result of his stay in India will be that he will have imparted a new breath of inspiration to Indian Christianity.

I next come to my old college contemporary, Lord Minto. To most of us he is better known as Melgund, to some of us as Rowley. Lord Minto's position raises in my mind a controversy which has never ceased to rage in it since I was thirteen years old. I have never been able to make out which has the greatest share in the government of this Empire—Scotland or Eton. I am quite prepared to give up our fighting powers to Ireland, because when we have from Ireland Wolseley and Kitchener and Roberts I am sure that Scotland cannot claim to compete. But when, as in Lord Minto's case, Scotland and Eton are combined, you have something so irresistible that it hardly is within the powers of human eloquence to describe it. Lord Minto comes of a governing family—indeed, at one time it was thought to be too governing a family. Under former auspices it was felt that the Elliots perhaps bulked too largely in the administration of the nation. At any rate, whether it was so or not, it was achieved by their merits, and there has been a Viceroy Lord Minto already. There have been innumerable distinguished members of the family in the last century, and there has also been a person, I think, distinguished above all others—that Hugh Elliot who defeated Frederick the Great in repartee at the very summit of his reputation, and went through every adventure that a diplomatist can experience. And now Lord Minto goes to Canada. I am quite certain, from his experience, from his character and knowledge, from his popularity, that he is destined to make an abiding mark.

Lastly, I take the case of our friend who is going to undertake the highest post of the three, because, after all, it is one of the highest posts that any human being can occupy. He goes to it in the full flower of youth, and of manhood, and of success—a combination to which every one must wish well. Lord

ADDRESSES

Curzon has this additional advantage in his favour—that he is reviving a dormant class, the Irish peerage. Some might think that that implied some new legislative or constitutional development on the part of her Majesty's Government, but it would be out of my place to surmise that to be the case. But, at any rate, sure I am of this—that Lord Curzon of Kedleston has shown in his position at the Foreign Office qualities of eloquence, of debating power, of argument, which have hardly been surpassed in the career of any man of his standing. I cannot say—it would be difficult to say—that he has done so in defence of difficult positions, because that would be at once to raise a political issue of the very gravest kind. But I am quite sure that no Under-Secretary has ever had to defend in the House of Commons any but positions of difficulty, and I think the foreign situations are always of that character. I am quite sure that when Lord Curzon has had to defend these situations he has defended them with not less than his customary success. He has devoted special study to India. I believe he has even entered into amicable relations with neighbouring potentates. He will pass from his home of Kedleston in Derbyshire to the exact reproduction of Kedleston in Government House, Calcutta. We all hope that in his time India may enjoy a prosperity which has of late been denied to her, and that immunity from war and famine and pestilence may be the blessed prerogative of Lord Curzon's Viceroyalty.

I have only one word more to say before I sit down, and it is this—I think we all must have in our minds, at least some of us must have in our minds, some immortal words on the occasion of this gathering so interesting and even so thrilling. Do you all remember the beginning of the tragedy of "Macbeth"? The first witch says:

> "When shall we three meet again,
> In thunder, lightning, or in rain?"

The second witch replies:

> "When the hurly-burly's done,
> When the battle's lost and won."

Surely these significant words must be present

to us to-night. You are sending out three eminent men on three vitally important missions to different parts of the Empire. Two of them, at any rate, go for periods of five years, and we must think even in this moment of triumph and of joy of the period of their return, "When shall we three meet again?" That must be in their minds too; but this at least we may be sure of: if we are here present, or some of us, to greet them on their return when the hurly-burly's done and when the battle is not lost—for we exclude that—when the battle is won, they will have a tale of stewardship which is nobly undertaken and triumphantly achieved, one which has helped to weld the Empire which we all have it at heart to maintain, one which will redound to their own credit, and which will do if even but a little—for there is so much to be added to—to add to the glory and the credit of our mother Eton. I propose the health of Lord Minto, Lord Curzon, and the Rev. J. E. C. Welldon.

THE HAPPY TOWN COUN-
CILLOR

When Lord Rosebery, on October 30th, 1894, went to Bristol to unveil the statue of Burke (see page 4), the city seized the opportunity to make him a Freeman. In saying "Thank you" for the honour and the accompanying silver casket, Lord Rosebery (with distinct appropriateness) sang the praises of Civic as constrasted with Parliamentary life. He had himself at that time been Prime Minister a little more than six months; he has recently become an Epsom Urban District Councillor. The resultant pump can only be a matter of time.

THE HAPPY TOWN COUNCILLOR

I AM not a member of the House of Commons, and I never have been a member of the House of Commons; but I confess when I attempt to imagine what that existence can be I am bound to say that in every respect, so far as I can judge, a business man, a man who is fond of his home and of the life of home, and who wishes to see something tangible accomplished by his own work and his own exertions, would infinitely prefer the career of a municipal councillor to that of a member of the House of Commons. You smile, but what, after all, is the career of a member of the House of Commons as judged by the life outside? After an election of an agonising character he may or may not be elected to

ADDRESSES

serve his country in Parliament. If he be elected after a Session of the greatest exhaustion he employs his vacation, if he has a vacation at all, in travelling from village to village, or from ward to ward of his constituency, repeating a speech or repeating speeches which must become distasteful to himself and cannot be otherwise than distasteful to those who hear him. At the end of that recess, if recess there be, he is called back to his Parliamentary duties in London. For that he forsakes his home, forsakes his wife, forsakes his family, and if he have a business he becomes a sleeping partner in it. If he is a landlord he becomes an absentee, and for what? He sits on a bench in the House of Commons. He is conscious of ability and of powers of speech practised in the way I have described, but he is told by his Whip that on no account must he address the House though the debate, all the arguments in which he knows could be perfectly well exhausted in two hours, be prolonged for four or five days. During those days he witnesses the rising of right hon. friends and

THE HAPPY TOWN COUNCILLOR

opponents on the front benches to make their speeches, and also of those irresponsible bores whom no Whip and no Minister can soothe to silence. There he sits, conscious that if he had to do it all he could do it so much more ably, and then finally he is whisked away to the lobby, there to vote as he is told to vote.

On the other hand, what is the life of a town councillor? He lives in his home in a town to which he is accustomed. He is able to look after his business, to see his wife, and control the education of his children, and two or three times a week he goes to attend a practical piece of public work, the practical results of which he will see in his own lifetime. I do not wish to say anything disrespectful of members of Parliament, more especially in the presence of Sir Michael Hicks-Beach and other gentlemen here, but I do believe from the bottom of my heart that a man who is a town councillor can effect in his term of office some small, practical, and tangible good, such as even the erection of a pump, and at the end of his term of office he

ADDRESSES

has something infinitely more tangible and satisfactory to look upon than has a member of Parliament. He sees his pump ; he sees the water flow; and he sees the monument of what he has done, and knows he has contributed to the health, welfare, and, possibly, the sanitation of his neighbours. But at the end of the Parliamentary Session what has the ordinary member of the House of Commons got to look at that can be compared with that ? At any time the town councillor may rise to the position which you, Mr. Mayor, so worthily occupy. In that position he is looked upon by all his fellow citizens with respect, without envy, with a cordial wish to assist him in the discharge of his functions ; and he is the undisputed chief of the community. But what is the future of the ambitious member of the House of Commons ? It may be that ultimately, if his wildest dream be realised, he will become a Minister. There I draw the veil. The happiness of a career that has its culmination in becoming a Minister needs no criticism.

SPORT

In 1897 Lord Rosebery's bay filly, Mauchline, won the Gimcrack Stakes at York August Meeting. One consequence of this was that later in the year (on December 7th) Lord Rosebery, as the owner of the winning horse, had to reply (as he did in the following Address) to the toast of his health at the annual dinner of the York Race Committee and the Brethren of the Ancient Fraternity of York Gimcracks. The actual form of the toast proposed by Lord Wenlock was: " Success and perpetuity to the Gimcrack Club, coupled with the name of the Earl of Rosebery, the owner of Mauchline." It is notorious that Lord Rosebery's success in " classic " races has been the occasion of some controversy. His own observations on the point, written when he was Prime Minister in June 1894, should not be forgotten: " Like Oliver Cromwell," he said, " whose official position was far higher than mine, and the strictness of whose principles can scarcely be questioned, I possess a few race horses, and am glad when one of them happens to be a good one."

SPORT

I FIND myself compelled to respond, or honoured by responding, for the club which I meet to-night for the first time, and with which therefore I cannot be so intimately acquainted as some of you; but there is another difficulty still. I have won this race three times in my life, but I do not ever remember being asked to dinner before. Whatever be the cause, it is only of recent years that I have become acquainted with the dinner of the Gimcrack Club, and what makes my task more difficult is that I understand that, owing to the precedents of late years— the Gimcrack Club having been in relation to the Turf very much the same as the Lord Mayor's dinner stands in relation to politics— it is given to the guest of the evening to

ADDRESSES

deliver himself of some dissertation on current turf matters, and to offer suggestions for some violent reform. Of that I am quite incapable. If you welcome me here under those pretences, I must tell you at once I am an impostor. I very seldom go to races, and if I go to see a particular race I usually arrive not long before the race takes place, and go very soon after it has taken place. As regards the rules of the Jockey Club, there was a time when I used to know something about them, but they have been so changed and modified since that I am informed by experts there are only two people who, in the belief of the most credulous, have any thorough acquaintance with them. One is Mr. Wetherby and the other is Mr. James Lowther, and I am not perfectly sure of Mr. James Lowther.

In those circumstances it is a matter of embarrassment to know what I am to say to you to-night. I cannot extol the merits of the animal which won the Gimcrack Stakes, to which I am indebted for this honour, because, except on the occasion when she won this historic event, she has displayed no marked

SPORT

excellence, and offers no prospect of it. But, after all, I can always give advice with the perpetual prerogative of a person who has nothing to say. I am a little alarmed, I confess, at the juvenile reminiscences of my friend Lord Wenlock, because I am afraid that it may encourage my sons to take in their turn to racing. If I am asked to give advice to those who are inclined to spend their time and their money on the turf, I should give them the advice that *Punch* gave to those about to marry—"Don't." That, I admit, is a discouraging remark for an assembly of sportsmen, and I perceive that it is received in the deadest silence. I will give you my reasons for that remark. In the first place, the apprenticeship is exceedingly expensive; in the next place, the pursuit is too engrossing for any one who has anything else to do in this life; and, in the third place, the rewards, as compared with the disappointments, stand in the relation of, at the most, one per cent. An ounce of fact is worth a ton of exhortation, and I will give you my experience; and it will be an exceedingly genial

ADDRESSES

and pleasant dinner if everybody truthfully gives us his.

I will give you my experience of the Turf, and you shall judge whether I have not some foundation for the advice that I give. A great many years ago—too many years ago from one point of view—and at an early age—much too early an age from every point of view—I conceived the ambition to win the Derby. For a quarter of a century I struggled. Sometimes I ran second, sometimes I ran third, very often I ran last; but at last the time arrived when, as Lord Wenlock reminded you, I was about to realise the fruition of my hopes. I was with the second Ladas about to win the Derby, and I ought to have been the happiest of men. Well, after a quarter of a century of fruitless expectation, I won the Derby. But what was the result? I at that time held high office, as Lord Wenlock has also reminded you, under the Crown. I was immediately attacked from quarters of an almost inspired character for owning race-horses at all. With very little knowledge of the facts, and with much less of that charity

SPORT

that "thinketh no evil," I was attacked with the greatest violence for owning a racehorse at all. I then made the discovery, which came to me too late in life, that what was venial and innocent in the other officers of the Government—in a Secretary of State or a President of the Council, for example—was criminal in the First Lord of the Treasury. I do not even know if I ought not to have learnt another lesson—that although, without guilt and offence, I might perpetually run seconds and thirds, or even run last, it became a matter of torture to many consciences if I won.

But my troubles did not end there. Shortly afterwards we had a general election, and I then found that, having received abundant buffets on one cheek from the smiter, I was now to receive them on the other. I was then assailed, or rather those associated with me were assailed, not because we were too sporting, but because we were not sporting enough. Leagues and associations with high-sounding names and unerring principles were started to attack my unfortunate supporters, on the ground that we were not supporters of sport, I having already suffered so severely from having been too much a sportsman. I say then I have a right to give advice, having suffered on both sides for being too sporting and for not being sporting enough. That is my experience. I then hoped that my troubles were over. I withdrew into the sanctity of private life, and I felt that then, at any rate, fortune could no longer assail me, and that I should be enabled to pursue what I believe is facetiously called "the sport of Kings" without any particular detriment. But here again I am mistaken. Last year I thought, as so many of us have thought, that I possessed the horse of the century, and I believe that I did own a very good horse until he was overtaken by an illness; but I at once began, as foolish turfites do, to build all sorts of castles in the air—to buy yachts and to do all sorts of things that my means on that hypothesis would permit. From the very moment I began to form these projects the curse fell upon me. From October 1, 1896, to October 1, 1897, I ran second in every great race in which I ran, except two, which I won, and I think that, when I advise those who are about to race not to do so, I am justified by the experience which I have laid before you in so harrowing a manner.

Is there no compensation to those who pursue a sport which is carried on under such difficulties? I myself am of opinion that there are friendships formed and a knowledge of the world formed on the Turf which are invaluable to any man who wishes to get on in life. There was a famous lady who lived in the middle of this century, Harriet, Lady Ashburton, who summed up her views on the subject in a remark which has been preserved by the late Lord Houghton. She said, " If I were to begin life again I should go on the Turf merely to get friends. They seem to me to be the only people who really hold together—I do not know why. It may be that each man knows something that would hang the other, but the effect is delightful and most peculiar." If that was the cause of Turf friendship, the effect would be most peculiar; but of this I am perfectly certain that is not the real basis of Turf friendship.

ADDRESSES

I know nothing that would hang any of those I have known on the Turf, and I am quite sure that if anybody on the Turf, or if anybody had known anything that would hang me about three years ago, I should not be in life at this moment. But there must be more than friendship—more than secrets which are too dangerous for people to carry about with them—to constitute the real bond of union on the Turf.

Of course, many men say that it is gain. I do not think anybody need pursue the Turf with the idea of gain, and I have been at some trouble to understand why I and others, under singular difficulties, have pursued this most discouraging amusement. I see my trainer looking at me from a distant table with an inquiring eye. He could tell you probably better than I could tell you ; but, so far as I am concerned, the pleasures of the Turf do not so much lie on the racecourse. They lie in the breeding of a horse, in that most delightful furniture of any park or enclosure—the brood mare and the foal—in watching the development of the foal, the growth of the horse, and the exercise of the horse at home; but I do not believe that even that would be sufficient, if we had not some secret ambition to lure us on. It is obviously not in being winners of the Ten Thousand Guineas and such races, for these are practically unapproachable; but after very careful analysis from all the facts that have come under my observation, I believe it to be an anxious desire of aspirants for fame connected with the Turf to become the owner of what is called " the horse of the century."

Whether they will ever do so or not is a matter of very great doubt in all their minds, and how they are to set about it must be a matter of still more anxious inquisition. There is the method of purchase, but I speak in the presence of a number of gentlemen, some of whom perhaps breed horses for sale or have horses for sale, and I therefore do not venture to speak of that method with disparagement; but I do not think the horse of the century will ever be acquired at auction. Then there is the method of abstract theory and historical law. There is an idea that by

ADDRESSES

some connection with Byerley Turk—which in itself has a horrible flavour of the Eastern Question about it—that you may acquire the horse of the century. Lastly, there is the method of numbers — that new-fashioned method of numbers. You do something on paper that looks like a rule-of-three sum, and in a moment you have the horse of the century. I am not sure that we do believe in any of these ways. I believe the goddess of Fortune plays a great part in the production of the horse of the century. What we who are striving to produce that miraculous animal can fold to our bosom is this, that the century is drawing to a close, and that possibly we may have better luck in producing it in the twentieth century than we had in producing it in the nineteenth. There was a relative of mine, whose name may have been known to some of you as an eccentric lady, who lived in the East—I mean Lady Hester Stanhope. She also dreamed of having a miraculous animal of this description. She expected to possess a mare which should be born with a back like a saddle, which

SPORT

should carry a prophet into Jerusalem with Lady Hester by her side. She obtained the horse, but the prophet never arrived. And across all these dreams of the future there is one cloud in the horizon. We fancy that we feel the sobering influence of the motor-car. As yet it is only in its infancy, it is, as yet, rather given to afford a mild sensation of notoriety to its patrons, combined with a considerable smell of oil and a rattle of wheels. We may not yet imagine Lord Lonsdale hunting the Quorn hounds or inspecting a foreign army from the back of a motor-car. We may not yet be able to realise his Royal Highness the Prince of Wales leading home the victorious locomotive in the national race on Epsom Downs. Let us hope, at any rate, for the best. I believe that so long as institutions like the Gimcrack Club are kept in full vigour and are not allowed to die out we have a fair prospect of racing before us.

I must say one word in conclusion about the toast committed to my charge. It is that of the Gimcrack Club, and I see opposite me

ADDRESSES

an engraving of the picture, which I am so fortunate as to possess, by Stubbs of that very beautiful little animal. I am not quite sure why it is that the Gimcrack Club was founded, and founded in York, because as a matter of fact I looked over his performances this morning and I find that out of his very few defeats two of them took place on York race-course and his victories were usually in the south of England. We can never account for these things, and it is at any rate a great thing to have kept alive the memory of that gallant little horse—which, I do not suppose, stood over fourteen hands when alive—for nearly a century and a half in this ancient and venerable city. He was a horse which I think anybody would fear to possess now, with the conditions that he was to run two or three four-mile heats every week for £50; yet having been so valuable and admired as to found a club of his own, he constantly changed hands, and was once even allowed to become the possession of a foreigner. That, I think, is perhaps a danger that we escape. There must have been heavy hearts in York when Gimcrack became the property of a Frenchman. But he was reclaimed and lived to a good old age, and so has immortalised himself. But let me draw one concluding moral. This is the 131st dinner of the Gimcrack Club. He lived 130 years ago. How many poets, how many philosophers, aye, how many statesmen, would be remembered 130 years after they had lived? May we not draw from this fact the conclusion that the sport that we honour to-night, which we believe was never better and purer than at this moment, never more honest in its followers, never pursued with greater interest for the honour, as apart from the lucre, of the Turf, may we not draw this conclusion—that this sport will not perish in our land whatever its enemies may do, and that, however festive its celebration to-night may be, a century hence our descendants will be toasting the Gimcrack Club and hailing what I hope will be a more reputable representative of the winner of the Gimcrack Stakes?

GOLF

x

Lord Rosebery has not himself been swept away by what has been called the " Great Golf Stream "; but he has, at all events, allowed himself to be publicly identified with the game. On May 11th, 1897, he took part in the opening of the Edinburgh Burgess Golfing Society's Club House at Barnton, near Dalmeny. At the east entrance to the Club House he was presented with a gold key by the Captain of the Club, to which he responded by the first of these Addresses. The second was delivered at the consequent Cake and Wine Banquet, when, after the toast of "The Queen," Lord Rosebery was made an Honorary Member, and presented with a set of golf clubs. But though you may take a horse down to the water, you cannot make him drink.

GOLF

I

WHEN I was first asked in a cordial and pressing manner to take the leading part on this occasion, I rather thought that a trap was being laid for me, because I am so innocent of golf and all its works. I could not help dreading that the authorities of the club had determined that out of the mouth of complete innocence should come a testimony to the merits of golf, and that for that reason they had called upon one of the only Scotsmen who does not play the game to perform the ceremony. I did think that I was the only Scotsman with that unfortunate disability, but I have since learned that a great ecclesiastical authority, who lives at the very Mecca and shrine of golf itself—I mean St. Andrews

ADDRESSES

and I mean Dr. Boyd—although he has lived there for so many years, is completely innocent of the game. I wish you had taken Dr. Boyd instead of myself to dilate on the virtues of a game of which he must have seen a great deal more than I have ; but I was reassured by finding that I was not asked either as a golfer or as the reverse, but simply as a neighbour, to come and perform a neighbourly function in a neighbourhood which I know and which I love so well. I am sure that we of the neighbourhood, speaking to you as invaders of our serene quietude, can only express the most unbounded gratitude for the invasion. You have, in the first place, secured to the eyesight of the passer-by a beautiful and parklike space of land commanding glorious views of the Forth ; you have, in the next place, raised a building of which I can say truthfully and sincerely that it is an ornament to the neighbourhood and a credit to Mr. Cameron, the architect who has had the designing of it ; and, thirdly and lastly, you have infused into us a little life. We were an excellent neighbourhood, but we

GOLF

were a trifle dull perhaps. I think your golf links, and the railroad which accompanies it —I do not know whether it preceded or followed your golf club—have brought life into our midst, and on all those grounds I, speaking as a neighbour, as an unprejudiced neighbour, thank the golf club most heartily for setting up this pavilion in our midst.

II

I AM sincerely indebted to you for the honorary ticket of membership and for the set of golf clubs that you have been so good as to present to me. I should be very glad to think that the membership would cease to be honorary, and that I might be able to take my part in the amusements of the club, but I think that would require very mature consideration. In the meantime, at any rate, I shall preserve the book and the clubs as the trophy and memorial of an agreeable meeting. And, even if I were unable to make use of the clubs myself, there are two young gentlemen with whom I am connected and for whom I am responsible who, I think, would very likely take them off my hands if I neglected to make use of them. In correspondence with the secretary of the club he told me that he hoped I would make a short speech under the verandah—to which I willingly acceded

GOLF

—but that my principal speech would be made upstairs. I rejoined that I did not propose on this occasion to make any principal speech, because it struck me as an occasion of a neighbourly, friendly, and informal kind, and I think I should dissipate all the charm of the meeting if I were to laboriously get up a speech on golf from one of the popular handbooks and deliver a lecture amid the covert smiles of my audience.

After all, however, it is not uninteresting to know what are the impressions of the pursuit, with which you are thoroughly conversant, when regarded from an outside point of view—and I myself, of course, am only an outsider; but I do say one special recommendation of golf — a recommendation which will increase on me as I grow older — is that it is a game that can be pursued to an advanced period of life. In that respect it is like the royal game of tennis—the illustrious game of tennis. But then tennis is a game that has very few facilities of the courts for playing it, whereas

ADDRESSES

golf requires very little but assisted nature for its development. I am told that the game of fives is also a game that can be practised in extreme old age, but I suspect that those who try to carry out that theory will find that the game of fives, like the highest statesmanship of Europe, requires an iron hand within a velvet glove, and I for one should be very sorry to expose my hand to the game of fives with the slightest hope of being able to write a letter for many weeks afterwards. It is, I think, a very leading advantage of the game of golf, but of course it is an advantage which has, I suppose, secured to a large extent its universal popularity. Scotland has once more now conquered the world by her game of golf. There is no common in England which is so lonely or so deserted as not to expose to view two gentlemen followed by a couple of boys with a bundle of clubs. In my own neighbourhood of Surrey, where I am quite certain that golf was never heard of till ten or twelve years ago, our walks abroad are rendered almost as dangerous as the

GOLF

facing of a battery in time of war by the enormous number of metropolitan golfers who hurry down to enjoy their favourite pursuit.

That would seem almost to be a sufficient praise in itself, but I think there is a very considerable drawback, and at the risk of being torn to pieces before I leave this room I will mention what the drawback is. The other day I was speaking to an old friend of mine—tortures shall not wring his name from me, because his life would not be safe. He said, "I hear you are going to open a golf clubhouse next week. I wonder at that, because I always thought it a very dull game." My censure and criticism of golf is at the other pole to that of my friend. My dread of learning it, my dread of coming among you as an actual member is this, that it is far too engrossing and absorbing. When a man is once seriously inoculated with the love of golf he is of very little use for other pursuits of society. I know one gentleman at least of considerable possessions and large business transactions

ADDRESSES

who declines to open his letters on the morning on which he is going to play golf for fear anything in them should distract his attention; and a short time ago, without trenching on the strict barrier that divides us happily from politics to-day, I saw it as a charge against a distinguished statesman that he gave too much time to golf and not enough to the House of Commons. I say, then, when a man in middle life makes a deliberate choice of golf as his amusement, knowing these facts and viewing the infatuation of his friends, he is making a choice second only in gravity to the choice of a wife. I myself shrink, I am bound to say, without further knowledge, therefore, from becoming an actual member of your club, but for reasons I gave before I give you my most hearty good wishes for your welfare and prosperity, and I may at least avail myself of the privilege that you have conferred on me of inviting my guests to come and take a game over the links, and if so to watch as a dispassionate philosopher the progress of the game. I shall only gain in your esteem by

GOLF

not making myself a golfer actually and practically without a much longer and more serious consideration of the prospect that it involves.

INDEX

INDEX

ABERDEEN, Lord, 184, 292
"Accompt Book of Wedderburn, The," 273
Addington and Burns, 63
Addison, 67, 94, 157, 158
Æschylus, 158
Africa, 191
Althorp, 153
Angelo, Michael, 258
"Antiquary, The," 91
Ariosto, 163
Arlington Street, 126
Ascham, Roger, 155
Ashburton, Lady, 313
Atholl Crescent, Mr. Gladstone and, 115

BALFOUR, Mr. Arthur, 173
Bannockburn, 83
Baudelaire, 92
Beaconsfield, Lord, 23, 133, 254
Bell, Mr. Fitzroy, 275
Besant, Sir Walter, 123, 126
Bicycling, 236
Bismarck, 226
Black, Adam, 143
Blackie, Professor, 141

Blackstone, 158
Blaikie, Mr., 278
Blind Harry, 78
Bolingbroke, 67, 157, 163
  a bookish statesman, 153
BOOKISHNESS AND STATESMANSHIP, 141, *et seq.*: Reminiscences of the Philosophical Institution of Edinburgh, 141; the genius of Brougham, 144; Mr. Gladstone one of the most bookish statesman that ever lived, 145; Macaulay's literary avidity, 146; the life of the library and the life of politics, 147; the publicity of politics, 148; Mr. Gladstone a true lover of books, not a bibliomaniac, 149; his literary exports and imports, 151; the bookishness of Prime Ministers — Harley, 153; Bolingbroke, 153; Stanhope, 153; Sunderland, 153; Walpole, 153; Lord Grenville, 155; Canning, 156; Melbourne, 156; Sir Robert Peel, 156;

335

INDEX

Lord John Russell, 156; Lord Beaconsfield, 156; Lord Salisbury, 156; the bookishness of other Ministers—Addison, 157; Burke, 157; Charles Fox, 157; Chesterfield, 160; Carteret, 160; the last two centuries presenting no real parallel to Mr. Gladstone, 164; Mr. Parnell the exact antipodes of Mr. Gladstone, 166; the true life of the politician the balance of action and study, 168; bookishness a source of happiness to the statesman, 169

"Book of Dignities," Haydn's, 279

Boyd, Dr., 324

Braxfield, 179

Bright, John, 254

Bristol and Burke, 6

Bristol, the freemen of, 10

Brougham, Lord, 7, 143, 144, 178

Browne, Sir Thomas, 92

Browning, 92, 130

Bruce, 83

Burford Bridge, 90

BURKE, 6, *et seq.*: his connection with Bristol, 6; his meagre official honours, 7; reasons for losing his seat at Bristol, 8; the manufacture of Bristol freemen, 10; his connection with Chatterton, 11; secret of his character, 12; his views on reform, 13; his attitude towards the French Revolution, 14; his devotion to the call of duty, 16; use of his time out of office, 17; impeachment of Warren Hastings, 17; his comparative failure in his lifetime, 18; his eventual justification, 19; "what shadows we are," 20; his enduring fame, 21; his burial-place, 25; the unsuccessful farmer, 25; his rural surroundings at Gregories, 26; compounding pills for the poor, 26

Burke, 50, 157

Burney, Miss, 90

BURNS, ROBERT, 31, *et seq.*: his Dumfries associations, 31; Scotland's special debt to him, 33; the celebration of his death, 34; his last months, 36; his funeral, 39; "happy in the occasion of his death," 40; his last years of misery, 41; the best poetry produced before middle age, 44; his confidence in the judgment of posterity, 45; this confidence vindicated, 46; the reasons of his confidence, 47; his masterpiece, 47; his place in the roll-call of fame, 49; the Titans of the eighteenth century, 50; the secret of his fame, 51; "the miracle called Burns," 52; his early life, 52; the man far more wonderful than his works, 53; the magnetism of his presence and conversation, 54; his prose, 55; his sympathy, 56; the charm of the home, 56; the universality of his poetry, 57;

INDEX

his special claim on Scotsmen, 59; his inspired alchemy, 60; the patriot, 60; his relations with three Prime Ministers, 62; "A man's a man for a' that," 63; the lover, 63; a life of work and truth and tenderness, 64; his love affairs, 65; his conviviality, 66; his imperfections and weaknesses a comfort and a guide to erring humanity, 68
Burns, 85, 99, 130, 158, 195
Burton, John Hill and Wallace, 81
Byerley Turk, 316
"Byeways of Scottish History, The," 277
Byron, 130

CADE, Jack, 130
Cæsar, 84
Cameron, Mr., 324
Canada, 295
Canning, a bookish statesman, 156
Canning, 283
Carlyle, 143
Carlton Terrace, 126
Carteret, 160
Catherine II. of Russia, 75
Cavour, 84, 226
Chalmers, Dr., Mr. Gladstone and, 115
Chatterton, 11, 35
Chaucer, 92
Chesterfield, 160, 162
Chevening, 153
Churchill, Lord Randolph, and the Vote of Credit in 1885, 251

CIVIL SERVANTS, OUR, 207, et seq.: the two classes of officials, 208; those who make speeches and those who interpret them, 209; a concrete example, 210; a Civil Service strike, 211; the Vice-President of the Council, 214; the relations between the transient heads of office and their permanent occupants, 216
Civil Service, the, 192
Clarendon, 157
Clark, Mr., and Burns, 43
Clerihugh's, 180
Cobden, 254
Cockburn, Lord, 177
 "Memorials of his Time," 180
Cockpit, the, 125
Colonsay, Lord, 141
Colville, Mr. Henry, 277
Commons, House of, Lord Rosebery and, 301
Comyns, the, 78
Congreve, 93, 158
"Coningsby," 156
"Cottar's Saturday Night," 44
Cowper, 158
Crabbe and Burke, 26
Cromarty, Lord, and Burns, 59
Cruger and Burke, 9
Culloden, 278
Cunningham, Mr., and Burns, 41
Curzon, Lord, of Kedleston, 296

DALGETTY, Capt. Dugald, 159
Dalmeny, 144
Dante, 144, 163
Darien Scheme, the, 281

INDEX

Defoe, 92
Derby, the, 310
Dialectic Society, 177
"Dr. Jekyll and Mr. Hyde," 94
Dumfries and Burns, 31
Dunbar, 86
Duncan, Dr. Matthews, 142
Dundas, 18, 58, 185
Dunlop, Mrs., and Burns, 42
DUTY OF PUBLIC SERVICE, THE, 173, *et seq.*: The Associated Societies of the University of Edinburgh, 176; Edinburgh in 1787, 177; the inevitable disappearance of true originality, 178; the new Edinburgh and the old, 180; Edinburgh, the assiduous mother and foster mother of the builders of the Empire, 185; the British Empire rests on men, 186; the call to service an increasing one, 186; the claims of Parliamentary life, 187; the London County Council, 188; the Municipalities, 188; County Councils, District Councils, and Parish Councils, 189; the Government Departments, 189; British administration abroad, 191; the Diplomatic and Consular Services, 192; the Civil Service, 192; a general staff of the Empire, 193; the drain on the Treasury, 194; official duty only a very small part of public duty, 195; public spirit in the country never higher, 196; "What can I do, in however small a way, to serve my country?" 198; vigilance in public affairs the irreducible minimum of public service, 199; the basis of Empire, 200
"Dynamiter, The," 95

EDINBURGH, 180; its statues, 100; the Associated Societies of the University of, 176; an Imperial city, 203.
Edinburgh Review, the, 177
Elgin, Lord, 184
Elliot, Hugh, 295
Empire, the British, 186
"Endymion," 90
ENGLISH-SPEAKING BROTHERHOOD, THE, 261, *et seq.*: All territorial expansion justified by those who make it, 262; the adjective "Anglo-Saxon," 263; what constitutes race and nationality, 264; American independence, 264; history justifies its wisdom and expediency, 265; independence cements the racial bond, 266; the colonial development of European States, and its effect on Great Britain, 266; the partition of the world—and afterwards, 267; the next great war—for trade and not for territory, 268; the New World and the Old, 269
Erskine, Sir Thomas, and Burke, 18
Eskgrove, 179
ETON, 287, *et seq.*: A brilliant gathering, 287; Eton terri-

INDEX

tory, 289; dim and distant associations, 290; its playing fields, 291; its Imperial record, 292; the new Bishop of Calcutta, 293; the new Governor-General of Canada, 294; the new Viceroy of India, 295; "When shall we three meet again?" 297

Eton, 150, 153

Euripides, 158

FALKIRK, battle of, 77

Farrer, Lord, 213

Ferguson, 99

Fielding, 8, 158

Fives, 326

Fletcher of Saltoun, and Burns, 59

Flodden, 86

Florizel, Prince of Bohemia, 95

Football, 236

Fordun, 76

Fox, Chas. James, 16, 25, 50, 66, 93, 157, 168, 249, 250

Fox, Henry, 154

Francis, Sir Philip, and Burke, 14

Frederick the Great, 168, 295

Free libraries, 235

French Revolution, the, 14, 20 Burns and, 62

GEORGE III., 265

Gibbon, 158

Gibson-Craig, Sir William, 142

Gimcrack Club, the, 307, 317

GLADSTONE, 105, *et seq.*: His place in history, 105; his intellect and character, 106; his power of concentration, 107; the variety and multiplicity of his interests, 107; the universality and humanity of his sympathy, 108; the depth of his Christian faith, 110; his admiration of "manhood," 110; the four years of retirement before his death, 111; the solitary and pathetic figure of Mrs. Gladstone, 112; an animating and inspiring example, 114; his connection with Edinburgh, 115; the first Midlothian campaign, 116; a matchless individuality, 118

Various references, 24, 156, 163, 164, 250

President of the Philosophical Institution of Edinburgh, 143; the bookish statesman, 144-145; Midlothian campaign, 254

Gladstone, Mrs., 113

"Globe," the, 68

Goethe, 50, 68

Goldsmith, Oliver, 36

GOLF, 323, *et seq.*: The exceptions proving the rule that all Scotsmen golf, 323; its advantages, 327; its popularity, 328; the dangers of inoculation, 329

Gordon, Mr., 142

Gordon, the Duchess of, and Burns, 54

Granville, Lord, 287

Gray, 57

Gregories, 25

Gregory's powders, Dr., 32

Grenville, Lord, 161 a bookish statesman, 155

Grub Street, 131

INDEX

HAILES, Lord, and Henry II., 81
Hamilton, Single-speech, 258
Hamilton, Lady, 90
Hamilton, Sir Edward, 212
HAPPY TOWN COUNCILLOR, THE, 301, *et seq.*: Municipal and Parliamentary life compared, 301; the career of a member of the House of Commons, 302; the life of a town councillor, 303
Harley, a bookish statesman, 153
Harrison, Mr. George, 142
Harvey, Sir George, 142, 275
Hastings, Warren, and Burke, 17
Hatfield, 156
Hawes Inn, Queensferry, 90
Hawthorne, 92
Haydn's "Book of Dignities," 279
Hazlitt, 92
Hermand, 179
Hicks-Beach, Sir Michael, 303
Highland Mary, 65
Homer, 144, 157, 161, 165
Houghton, 154
Houghton, Lord, 313

INDIA, 134, 191, 294
Ireland, 190

JAMES II., 159, 277
Jeffrey, Lord, 177, 178, 181
Jenkinson, Colonel, and Burns, 62
Jockey Club, 308
Johnson, 124, 162
"Jolly Beggars," 45, 47
Jonson, Ben, 68

JUDGMENT, THE QUALITY OF—see QUALITY OF JUDGMENT, THE, 221, *et seq.*

KANDAHAR, 134
Keats, 90, 92
"Kidnapped," 91
Kitchener, Lord, 294

LADAS, 310
Lagado, Academy of, 63
Lamb, 92
Lewis, Sir George Cornewall, 146
LIBRARIES, THE WORK OF PUBLIC—see WORK OF PUBLIC LIBRARIES, THE, 235, *et seq.*
LONDON, 123, *et seq.*: Sir Walter Besant's contribution to London and its literature, 124; the historic associations of its streets, 124; the Cockpit, 125; where Governments are formed, 126; the identity of its historic houses, 127; proportionately more beautiful formerly, 128; the legend of Whittington, 128; the stepmother of literature, 129; a great and neglected problem, 132; the key of the British Empire, 134
London County Council, 127, 188
Long John, 97
Lonsdale, Lord, 317
Lords, House of, 77, 187
Lowther, Mr. James, 308
Lundin, Sir Richard, 80
Luther, 84

INDEX

MACAULAY, 143, 146; and the Philosophical Institution of Edinburgh, 144; his influence as a Parliamentary speaker, 253
"Macbeth," 297
Mannering, Col., 180
Mar, Lord, and Burns, 57
Marie Antoinette, 14
Marlborough, the Duke of, 255
Massinger, 158
Masson, Professor, 61
    and the University of Edinburgh, 175
"Master of Ballantrae," the, 96
M'Ewan, Mr., 173
Melbourne, a bookish statesman, 156
"Memoirs of a Highand Lady," 181
"Memorials of John Murray of Broughton, The," 274
Mercat Cross, Mr. Gladstone and the, 118
"Mermaid," the, 68
Metastasio, 158
Midlothian Campaign of 1879, 254
Millet, 35
Milner, Sir Alfred, 213
Milton, 155, 158
Minto, Lord, 184, 294
Mirabeau, 84
Moir, Dr., Blind Harry and, 79
Montaigne, 92
"Montreuil Correspondence," 273
More, Hannah, 150
Morley, Mr. John, and Burke, 5
Morris, 92
Mowatt, Sir Francis, 212

Mozart, 50
Municipal Service—*see* HAPPY TOWN COUNCILLOR, THE, 287, *et seq.*
"Murray of Broughton, Memorials of," 274
Musgrave, Sir Christopher, and Burns, 59
"Mysteries of Paris, The," 94

NAPOLEON, 50, 75, 168
Nelson, 50, 90
Nelson, Mr. Thomas, 230
"New Arabian Nights," the, 94
Newton, 179
North, Christopher, 143

OBERMAN, 92
Ockerby, Mr., 279
ORATORY, PARLIAMENTARY—*see* PARLIAMENTARY ORATORY, 247, *et seq.*

PALMERSTON, Lord, 156
PARLIAMENTARY ORATORY, 247, *et seq.*: The advantages and perils of the written speech, 248; the speeches of Pitt and Fox, 249; speeches which influenced votes—Mr. Gladstone, 251; a Liberal Peer, 252; Lord Macaulay, 253; Mr. Cobden, the most effective orator of his time, 254; the Midlothian campaign, 254; the effect of oratory in the United States, 255; the motive determines the value of Parliamentary eloquence, 255; a means to an end, 256;

INDEX

"Single-speech Hamilton," 258

Parnell, his distaste for books and learning, 166, 169

Patriotism, exaggerated, 75

Paul, Mr. Herbert, lecture on "Parliamentary Oratory," 247

Peel, Sir Robert, 156

People's Palace, 124

Pew, 97

Pitt, 18, 50, 54, 62, 68, 93, 112, 168, 190, 249

Pope, 158

Porteous mob, the, 281

Primrose, Mr. Bouverie, 142

PUBLIC LIBRARIES, THE WORK OF—see WORK OF PUBLIC LIBRARIES, THE, 235, et seq.

PUBLIC SERVICE, THE DUTY OF—see DUTY OF PUBLIC SERVICE, THE, 173, et seq.

Pulteney, 159

Punch, 309

QUALITY OF JUDGMENT, THE, 221, et seq.: A rare quality, 224; the newspaper view the view of the moment, 225; Cavour and Bismarck, 226; judgment obtained by intercourse with one's fellow men and by reading, 227; newspapers and books, 228; the free library an inexhaustible boon, 230

Quarter Sessions, 187

Queensberry, the Duke of, 61

RACING, 307

Reynolds, Sir Joshua, 258

Riddell, Mrs., and Burns, 37, 41, 43

Roberts, Lord, 294

Robertson, Principal, and Burns, 55

"Robinson Crusoe," 97

Roman Catholic Emancipation, 20

Roumania, Queen of, 59

Ruskin, 92

Russell, Lord John, 156

ST. ANDREWS, 323

St. Deiniol and Mr. Gladstone, 150

St. James's Square, 124

Salisbury, Lord, 156 and Mr. Gladstone, 106

Salisbury, Lady, and Mr. Gladstone, 109

Samoa, 101

Sanderson, Sir Thomas, 210

Sarpedon, 161

Savage, 124

Schiller, 50

"Scots Brigade, The Papers relating to the," 273

Scott, Sir Walter, 91, 130, 181, 195, 274

SCOTTISH HISTORY, 273, et seq.: The publications and work of the Scottish History Society, 273; the history of the Stuart family after the abdication of James II., 277; the history of Scotland in the eighteenth-century, 281; a "kodak" view of our own times, 284

"Scottish History, The Byeways of," 277

Scottish History Society, The, 284

INDEX

Seymour, Sir Edward, and Burns, 59
Shackleton, Miss, and Burke, 26
Shakespeare, 35, 52, 66, 68, 129, 158
Shelley, 130
Solemn League and Covenant, the, 85
Sophocles, 158
Southey, 130
Spectator, the, 94
SPORT, 307, *et seq.*: Turf reform and the Jockey Club rules, 308; advice to those about to take to the turf, 309; the lessons of experience, 309; the penalties of success, 310; the misery of running second, 312; turf friendship a compensation, 313; the amusements of the turf do not lie on the racecourse, 314; "the horse of the century," 315; the Gimcrack Club and its founder, 317; the vitality of sport, 319
Stanhope, a bookish statesman, 153
Steele, 94
Stephen, Sir Fitzjames, 215, 216
Stephen, Sir James, 215
STEVENSON, ROBERT LOUIS, 89, *et seq.*: Burford Bridge and the Hawes Inn, 90; his style, 92; his spirit of irony, 93; his dramatic, realistic power of imagination, 95; "the Master of Ballantrae" 96; "Treasure Island," 97; the need of memorials, 98;
the two passions of his life, 102
Stewart, Dugald, 178
and Burns 54, 56
Stirling, battle of, 77, 86
Stuart, Charles Edward, 66
Stuarts, the, 277
Sunderland, a bookish statesman, 153
Swift, 95
Swinburne, 92

TACITUS, his epitaph on Agricola, 40
Talleyrand, 90
"Tam o' Shanter," 32, 44
Tasso, 163
Tatler, the, 94
Tennis, 327
Tennyson, 130
Thackeray, 93, 95
Theocritus, 159
Thomson, Burns and, 37
Thurlow, 141
"To Mary in Heaven," 32
"Treasure Island," 97

UNITED STATES, the, 266
United States Presidentia election, the, 255

VANBRUGH, 158
Virgil, 158

WALDSTEIN, Professor, lecture on "The English Speaking Brotherhood," 261
Wales, Prince of, 317
Walking-sticks, 97
WALLACE, 73, *et seq.*: His nationality, 74; the few facts of his career, 76; his portentous,

INDEX

meteorical, providential appearance, 76; the biography of Blind Harry, 78; a man of the people, 80; a man of vast political and military genius, 81; a source of inspiration to his countrymen, 82; his legacy to Scotland, 83; the man of destiny, 84; his services to Scotland a service to the whole Empire, 86

Wallace, Mr., and Burns, 64

Walpole, 159
    a bookish statesman, 154

Washington, 84

Waterloo, 291

Wauchope, General, 117

Webster, 92

"Wedderburn, The Accompt Book of," 273

Welby, Lord, 213

Welldon, Rev. J. E. C., 293

Wellington, the Duke of, 50, 213, 291

Wenlock, Lord, 309

Wetherby, Mr., 308

"What shadows we are," 20

Whittington, Dick, 128

Wolseley, Lord, 294

Wood, Sir Evelyn, 207

Wordsworth, 92, 130

Wordsworth and Chatterton, 12

WORK OF PUBLIC LIBRARIES, THE, 235, *et seq.*: The predominance of outdoor sport, 235; muscle and brains, 237; the art of thinking, 238; the Press an enemy of independent thinking, 238; public libraries a counter-irritant to intellectual apathy, 240; the difficulty of selection in reading, 241; the librarian as a "taster" of books, 242

www.ingramcontent.com/pod-product-compliance
Lightning Source LLC
Chambersburg PA
CBHW020245240426
43672CB00006B/645